BALLET DESIGN

PAST & PRESENT

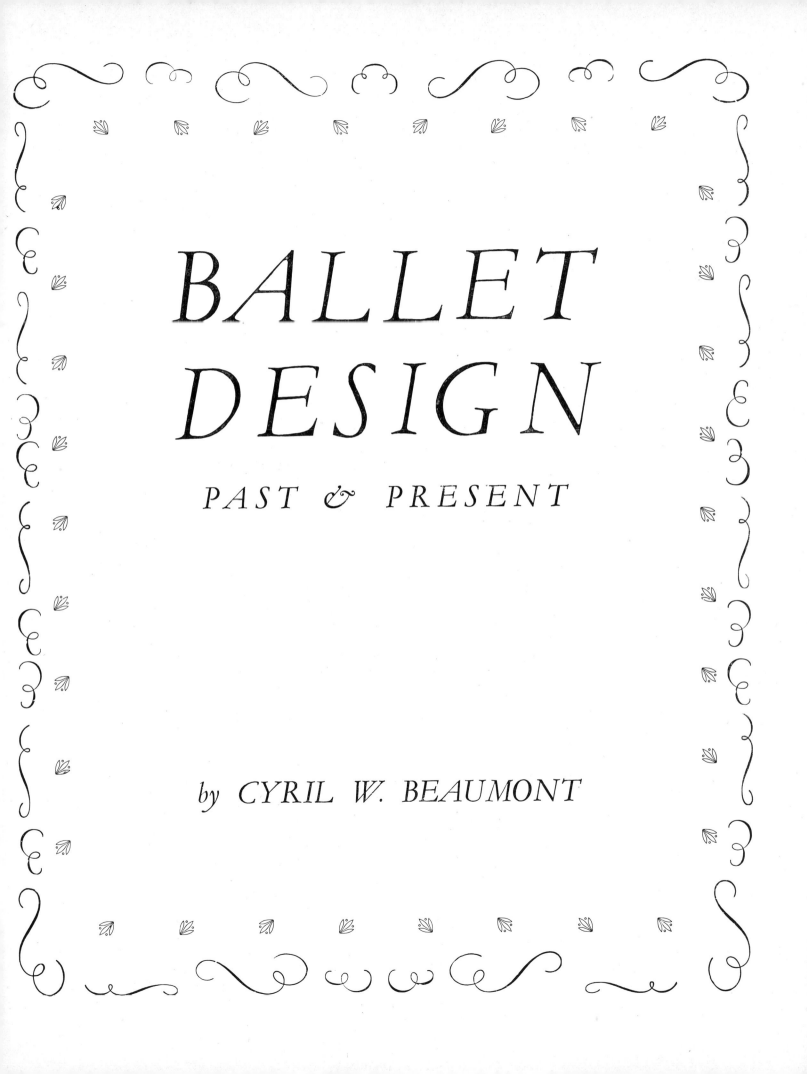

BALLET DESIGN

PAST & PRESENT

by CYRIL W. BEAUMONT

First published in this form 1946

ACKNOWLEDGMENTS

In assembling material for the illustration of this book the Author wishes to record his deep indebtedness to his friends, Doris Niles and Serge Leslie, who most generously placed at his disposal their splendid collection of prints and engravings relating to the Ballet; moreover, the latter placed the writer still further in his debt by carrying out certain research work on his behalf in the libraries of Paris.

The Author also desires to express his grateful thanks to the artists who have so kindly allowed their designs to be reproduced, and in particular to those who have lent original drawings for reproduction; and to record his deep appreciation of the courtesies afforded him by M. Rolf de Maré and Dr. Pierre Tugal, respectively Founder-Director and Curator of Les Archives Internationales de la Danse, Paris; M. J. G. Prod'homme, Curator of the Bibliothèque and Musée de l'Opéra, Paris; the Directors of the Exposition sur les Ballets Russes de Serge de Diaghïlev, Pavillon de Marsan, Paris; the staff of the Print Room, British Museum, London; the staff of the Department of Prints and Drawings, Victoria and Albert Museum, London; the Society for Cultural Relations with Foreign Countries, Moscow; Messrs. Tooth's Galleries, London—the designs by A. Benois being derived from their exhibition of that artist's work; His Grace the Duke of Devonshire; M. André Bakst; Col. W. de Basil; the late M. René Blum; Miss Derra de Moroda; M. Willson Disher, Esq.; Anton Dolin, Esq.; Ashley Dukes, Esq.; M. Paul Eltorp; Dr. Paolo Fabbri; M. Gyula Harangozò; Captain R. C. Jenkinson; Robert E. Jones, Esq.; Geoffrey Keynes, Esq.; Albert M. King, Esq.; Lincoln Kirstein, Esq.; Miss Joan Lawson; M. Serge Lifar; Miss Catherine Littlefield; Miss Ruth Page; P. R. Revitt, Esq.; Harold Rubin, Esq.; Sacheverell Sitwell, Esq.; *The Dance* Magazine, New York; Dr. Walter Toscanini and John V. Trevor, Esq. in connection with the loan of material.

Printed in England by Hazell, Watson & Viney, Limited, London and Aylesbury. Published in London by The Studio, Ltd., 66, Chandos Place W.C.2, and in New York by the Studio Publications Inc., 381, Fourth Avenue.

DESIGNERS

* Denotes Colour Plate.

* Denotes Colour Plate.

BALLET COMPANIES, COMPOSERS, CHOREOGRAPHERS, ETC.

INTRODUCTION

IN this volume I have combined and extended my two previous works on this subject, *Five Centuries of Ballet* and *Design for the Ballet*, in an attempt to trace the evolution of design for Ballet from the Italian Renaissance to the present day. Since the process of development is to be seen most clearly in France, the successive innovations effected at the Paris Opera will provide the main theme for this study, with occasional consideration of activities in other countries.

In its beginning, Ballet was essentially a costly entertainment devised by and for the aristocracy. It was the direct outcome of the Court entertainments which came into vogue during the fourteenth and fifteenth centuries and were especially popular in Italy. These entertainments were variously known as mummings (*momeries*), masquerades (*mascherate*), and interludes (*intermedii*).

The mumming was given by persons disguised and masked, who danced without mingling with the spectators ; sometimes the maskers appeared suddenly in the midst of an assembly, sometimes they made a more ceremonious entry on foot or in an allegorical car, preceded by torch-bearers and musicians. The masquerade consisted of a number of gaily decorated cars filled with actors in costume ; the procession filed past the personage it was desired to honour and, as each car stopped before him, the principal actor declaimed a laudatory poem or address. These cars presented a kind of *tableau vivant* placed on a decorated platform mounted on wheels, and were drawn by appropriately dressed persons or by gaily caparisoned horses. Such cars might represent the Chase—a party of hunters pursuing a stag ; the Four Seasons ; a Combat between knights and infidels ; or perhaps a Sea Piece, with tritons and naiads disporting amid the waves. That such conceptions were highly artistic in representation can be proved by an examination of some of the etchings by Callot after Stefano della Bella. The interlude was a little scene of dancing, singing, and mechanical effects given between the acts of a play or during a banquet.

A famous example of the interlude, which for all practical purposes may be regarded as the prototype of Ballet, was the splendid entertainment given at Tortona in 1489 on the occasion of the marriage of Galeazzo, Duke of Milan, and Isabel of Aragon. Devised by Bergonzio di Botta, it took the form of a banquet at which each dish was presented with an appropriate dance. The event became famous throughout Europe so that the smallest Court aspired to present similar entertainments.

There were also local masquerades such as the Florentine *Canti* and *Trionfi* which also influenced Court festivities. Here, the performers were masked and disguised in a rich and theatricalised version of costumes associated with familiar occupations ; for instance, shepherds, gardeners, fishermen, and the like. Then, accompanied by a band of musicians, the masquers danced through the streets singing gay songs appropriate to their assumed calling. Sometimes the spectacle acquired an additional piquancy by the men's wearing women's clothes. In the *Canti* the merrymakers went on foot, with torch-bearers to light their way ; in the *Trionfi* a number of allegorical cars were employed.

Italy exercised a great artistic influence on France. François I, during his expedition to Italy, was immensely impressed by the culture of the Italian Courts and engaged numbers of Italian painters, sculptors, and musicians to come to France and take part in the Court entertainments. The new fashion found an enthusiastic patron in Catherine de Medici who sponsored it at the Court of France as a diversion for her sons, François II, Charles IX, and Henri III, while she retained a firm grasp of the government. The most important of such spectacles was the *Ballet Comique de la Reine* (1581) which celebrated the betrothal of the Duc de Joyeuse to Marguerite de Lorraine, the Queen's sister. This work is fully described in a volume dated 1582 which incidentally is regarded as the first printed version of a ballet.

The author was a famous violinist, Baldasarino da Belgiojoso (later frenchified to Balthasar de Beaujoyeux), who came to France in 1555. He was presented to the Queen who appointed him *Valet de Chambre,* and later employed him in the capacity of unofficial organiser of Court festivals.

In his preface to the printed version of his ballet, Beaujoyeux defines ballet as " a geometrical mixture of many persons dancing together to the harmony of several instruments." The designation *ballet comique* means comedy-ballet, and the prime importance of Beaujoyeux's contribution is that he succeeded in dramatising the ballet, for dancing, music, singing, declamation and procession are dexterously combined for the expression of the theme, which was the tale of Circe. The entertainment, we are told, lasted from " ten o'clock in the evening until three and a half hours after midnight, nor did the length of it weary or displease the audience."

The ballet was given at the Salle du Petit Bourbon, Paris, a great hall with tiers of seats, in the form of galleries, erected on two sides ; the King and the Queen-Mother sat on a dais at the end of the hall. If the reader will glance at the plate on page 1, the scenic arrangement will be clear. It will be observed that there are three scenes. To the right is the Grove of Pan ; to the left is a gilded arch covered with gleaming clouds ; while, in the far distance, is Circe's Garden and Palace, with a passage either side for the entrance and exit of the decorated cars. I have described this setting at length because it presents an interesting application of the *décor simultané* or multiple setting encountered in the medieval mystery play.

Turning to a consideration of the costumes, which, like the setting, were designed by Jacques Patin, some idea of their splendour may be gained from Beaujoyeux's descriptions.

" Circe the enchantress was in a robe of gold tissue, of two colours, covered with little puffs of silk threaded with gold and overlaid with great silken veils threaded with silver. The ornaments on her head, and about her neck and arms, were marvellously enriched with precious stones and priceless pearls. In her hand she held a golden wand, five feet in length, just as legendary Circe used, to touch men in order to change them into animals or inanimate things.

" The Naiads were clothed in silver tissue covered with silver and crimson veils which billowed about the hips and all round the body, and everywhere at the ends were little puffs of crimson silk, threaded with gold, which added grace to the costume. Their leaders were adorned with little triangles enriched with diamonds, rubies, pearls, and other exquisite and precious stones. Their necks and arms were covered with necklaces, collarets, and bracelets, and all their clothing was covered with stones which shone and glittered as you see the stars appear at night in the blue vault of heaven. This adornment has been acclaimed to be the most superb, rich and pompous vestment ever seen in a masquerade."

Mention has already been made of Italian influence on the theatre and spectacle in France, an influence which, for that matter, spread to most countries. Now one of the main features of the Italian Renaissance was the revived interest in Graeco-Roman art and literature. Stage design received new inspiration from the rediscovery of the works of Vitruvius. These themes were developed in the *Architettura* (1551) of Sebastiano Serlio, and the *Practica di fabricar Scene e Machine ne' Teatri* (1631) of Nicola Sabbatini.

Serlio, following the teaching of Vitruvius, groups all settings under three heads : the Tragic, which demands a grandiose style, " columns, pedestals, statues and other objects suited to Kings " ; the Comic, which shows dwellings inhabited by the general public ; and the Satyric, which depicts cottages, trees, groves, arbours, and other objects of the countryside. The plan then was to provide a definite type of architectural background for the players according to the nature of the piece to be presented. It is important to stress the word *background*, because the players or dancers were intended to perform *before* the setting and not *in* it. In this resuscitation and adaptation of the *frons scaenae* characteristic of Graeco-Roman theatres, the stage designers of the Italian Renaissance laid the foundations of a school of grandiose architectural settings which was to attain its zenith in the eighteenth century under the Bibiena family and Piranesi.

This interest in an architectural background resulted in a study of the art and science of perspective, for had not Leonardo da Vinci declared that " Perspective is to Painting what the bridle is to a horse " ? Da Vinci, too, had interesting theories regarding the use of what he termed " aerial perspective," in which distance was not only suggested by perspective, but by the density of colouring of the several units which made up the complete setting, since the tone of an object varies with its distance from the spectator.

These architectural settings consisted of two-sided constructions representing buildings, ranged on either side of the stage, with a back-cloth painted in perspective. These buildings were light wooden frameworks covered with canvas painted in perspective. Such settings could also be used as a multiple setting, since various types of palaces or dwellings could be introduced, the action taking place before each in turn.

This type of setting, however, had the disadvantage in that the spectator became a little weary of gazing upon the same surroundings. Hence experiments were made with a view to devising simple means for effecting a change of scene. The conclusions reached are summed up in Sabbatini's work, which describes three methods of changing scenery: (a) by the use of the *periaktoi* of the Graeco-Roman theatre: mobile prisms, mounted longways on a pivot, so that they could be turned to present a **different face**, previously painted to depict a scene; (b) by the drawing of new canvases over the existing framework, and (c) by the provision of several two-sided painted screens which could be slipped in front of the first " house," and so present a new building. Finally, it was proposed that the back-cloth should be in the form of a shutter, each half of which could be withdrawn to its side to reveal a second scene or, if already drawn aside, could be closed over the original scene.

The representation of clouds was an important factor in spectacles founded on classic legend. These appear to have resembled a series of curved sky-borders, ranged one behind the other to suggest banks of clouds. These clouds became more and more elaborate as they were used in conjunction with the appearances, descents, and ascents of triumphal cars bearing illustrious deities.

Drop-curtains were rare, the change of scene being carried out in full view of the spectator, whose attention was to be diverted by means which can only be described as artless. For instance, Sabbatini suggests a staged disturbance at the back of the audience, or a sudden crash of drums and trumpets.

The lighting was obtained from candles or lamps hidden behind the scenery, or placed above the heads of the audience, and sometimes even on the stage itself in the manner of crude footlights. The intensity of the lighting was increased by placing bottles of water before the lights or setting burnished basins of brass or copper behind them. Coloured light was achieved by tinting the water in the bottles, an effect still to be observed in the windows of certain chemists' shops. As to effects, there were trap-doors for appearances and disappearances, while a person might be changed into a tree or a rock by the simple process of sliding up from below a piece of scenery so painted. There were devices for the simulation of lightning, while thunder was imitated by the rolling of a heavy cannon-ball over an uneven surface. Thunder played an important part in pieces in which deities abounded, since their appearance and departure were invariably marked by peals of thunder. Finally, the motion of seas was suggested by painted cloths caused to rise and fall by the turning of rollers placed beneath them, or by the manipulation of ropes attached to the under side of the cloths.

Among the several designers for the stage working in Italy during the late sixteenth and early seventeenth centuries may be mentioned Bernardo Buontalenti, Giacomo Torelli da Fano, Alfonso Parigi and Giulio Parigi.

In England the influence of Beaujoyeux's *Ballet Comique de la Reine* and of the experiments and achievements of Italian stage-designers, found its expression in masques, which were a popular form of entertainment at the Courts of James I and Charles I.

The most brilliant conceptions were those of Ben Jonson, the majority of whose masques were decorated by Inigo Jones. That architect was well acquainted with the progress of stage setting in Italy. Indeed a few of his designs show definite trace of the influence of the work of Alfonso and Giulio Parigi; but that is purely by the way, for Jones was a scenic artist of the first rank, who combined inspiration with practical knowledge, and continually experimented with new devices of his own conception throughout the thirty-five years (1605-1640) he was responsible for the staging of masques.

In Daniel's *Vision of Twelve Goddesses* (1605) he attempted to use *periaktoi* but found them too cumbersome, and so he experimented in turn with (a) the multiple setting, (b) the two-sided flats advocated by Sabbatini, with movable shutters at the far end of the stage, and (c) single-faced side-wings, each consisting of several units placed one behind the other in grooves, so that a change of scene could be effected by drawing back the flat facing the audience; in some productions there were as many as four; while the back-shutter, as in Davenant's *Salmacida Spolia* (1640), could also sometimes offer as many as four changes, and even the last shutter could be withdrawn to reveal a group of masquers in some particularly elaborate setting. The side-wings, following continental practice, diminished in height in accordance with the laws of perspective.

A particular feature of Jones's settings is a kind of decorative proscenium frame, embellished with appropriate figures and generally bearing a tablet inscribed with the name of the masque. Sometimes the scene was concealed by a curtain on which a landscape was depicted; sometimes the spectator's curiosity was excited by a mass of rock or clouds which masked the first setting.

Examine, for instance, the setting for Oberon's Palace in *Oberon* (1611). At the beginning of the masque there is nothing visible but a mass of rocks. The moon rises and shines on a portion of the rock, whence a satyr emerges and blows his horn. He is answered by another satyr, and still other satyrs come leaping out of the rocks. The satyrs decide to transfer their allegiance from Bacchus to Oberon. The rocky face parts to reveal the Palace of Oberon with two woodland creatures, dressed in leaves, sleeping before it, with clubs at their sides. The satyrs wake the sleeping guards, who inform them when the Palace gate will open. Presently the Palace parts, to reveal the land of fairies, some carrying lights, others musical instruments, while still others sing, and last of all there comes into view Oberon's chariot.

Lighting played a considerable part in Jones's productions and was evidently planned with careful regard for effect. For instance, Ben Jonson, describing the appearance of the masquers in *The Masque of Blackness* records that they " were placed in a great concave shell, like mother of pearl, curiously made to move on those waters and rise with the billow; the top thereof was stuck with a cheveron of lights, which indented to the proportion of the shell, struck a glorious beam upon them, as they were seated one above another, so that they were all seen, but in an extravagant order.

" On sides of the shell did swim six huge sea-monsters, varied in their shapes and dispositions, bearing on their backs the twelve torch-bearers, who were planted there in several graces; so as the backs of some were seen; some in purfle, or side; others in face; and all having their lights burning out of whelks, or murex-shells."

Again, in Samuel Daniel's *Tethys' Festival*, the poet, describing the discovery of Tethys and her nymphs, observes : " First at the opening of the heavens appeared three circles of lights and glasses, one within another, and came downe in a straight motion five foote, and then began to moove circularly; which lights and motion so occupied the eye of the spectators, that the manner of altering the Scene was scarcely discerned; for

in a moment the whole face of it was changed." Then, in describing the House of Fame, Daniel declares, " The Freezes, both below, and above, were fill'd with several-colour'd lights, like Emeralds, Rubies, Saphyres, Carbuncles, &c. the reflexe of which, with other lights, placed in the Concave, upon the Masquers habits, was full of glory." From these passages it is clear that Jones's lights were contained in coloured glasses, doubtless to ensure steady burning and as a precaution against fire.

And what of Jones's costumes? Here are some descriptions of those worn by Oceanus in Jonson's *The Masque of Blackness*, and of Boreas and Splendor in the same author's *The Masque of Beauty*.

" Oceanus presented in a human form, the colour of his flesh blue, and shadowed with a robe of sea-green; his head gray, and horned, as he is described by the ancients; his beard of the like mixed colour; he was gyrlanded with alga, or sea-grass; and in his hands a trident."

" Boreas, in a robe of russet and white mixt, full and bagg'd; his hair and beard rough and horrid; his wings gray and full of snow and icicles : his mantle borne from him with wires, and in several puffs : his feet ending in serpents's tails, and in his hand a leafless branch laden with icicles."

" Splendor, in a robe of flame-colour, naked-breasted, her bright hair loose flowing : she was drawn in a circle of clouds, her face and body breaking through : and in her hand a branch with two roses, a white and a red."

It will be noticed that Splendor is described as " naked-breasted," this is a physical characteristic of many of Jones's women's costumes, but whether the breasts were actually bared, or the gowns merely low-breasted, I am unable to say.

A popular costume for men, the first appearance of which it is difficult to establish, is that theatricalised version of the costume of a Roman warrior, a style known as *à la romaine*, which, as we shall see, remains the accepted dress for the dancer in the serious style until far in the eighteenth century. Many of the costumes have a certain androgynous quality—perhaps a gesture to James I—which makes it sometimes difficult to determine the sex of the masquer.

Thus, Ballet originated in Italy, was developed in France, to inspire the English masque, which in turn influenced the later French opera-ballets, which were the foundation of Ballet as an integral branch of the art of the theatre.

In France, from 1611 to 1651, that is to say during the reigns of Henri IV, Louis XIII, and the minority of Louis XIV, Ballet was one of the most popular diversions at the French Court. The majority of the ballets took their themes from classic legend, which led to the stage being peopled with gods, naiads, furies, dryads, tritons, and their kind; but now and again such poetical conceptions gave place to a degenerate form of ballet, in which buffoonery and the most grotesque fantasy ran riot. In such ballets women did not take part, the roles were taken by men dressed in women's clothes. The principal designer of costumes for the ballets produced at the Court of Louis XIII was Daniel Rabel (c.1578-1637) who had a fertile imagination and a rare gift for grotesque invention.

In *Les Femmes Renversées*, 1626, there were women with two faces, one showing a young woman, the other an old one; men who walked on all-fours with heads between their legs; dancers with heads placed at the height of their stomachs and covered with hats decorated with enormous plumes. In *La Douairière de Bille-bahaut* (1626), there were dancers who wore doublets reaching to their ankles, and others who were dressed in breeches which reached to their necks; there were drummers who marched each with a wooden leg—deformity, misfortune, crime, nothing came amiss as a subject for burlesque. In *Les Fées de la Forest de Saint-Germain* (1625) there was an *Entrée des coup-petestes* in which the dancers, armed with sword, club, or axe, wore false arms and hands, made of cardboard, which were struck off during the dance. Finally there were fantastic representations of the peoples of other countries, and costumes formed of articles associated with a particular calling, for instance, an innkeeper might have a dress composed of a barrel, a funnel, and a pair of pint pots.

The noblemen taking part in these ballets spent immense sums of money on their costumes, regardless of the nature of the character that might be allotted to them; for instance, a beggar would be clothed in torn clothes, yet made of the finest materials. But, whatever the nature of the ballet, and whether it was explained by words recited or sung, or by a series of dances, the sole purpose of the different *entrées* was to provide a suitable excuse for the entry of dancers wearing black or gold masks, and diadems adorned with tinselled aigrettes and plumes, who danced a number of figures generally containing some complimentary allusion. This particular set of dances was the recognised conclusion to every ballet and was known as the Grand Ballet. The dancers taking part in it were dressed alike in rich costumes resembling that *à la romaine*, the men usually in a tight-fitting jacket with short scalloped skirts of costly material which revealed the bare knee, the feet being incased in buskins reaching to the calf. The Grand Ballet was sometimes danced by ladies and sometimes by noblemen. But in the ballets in which the King and his courtiers appeared, no woman, of whatever rank, took part.

Louis XIV inherited his father's passion for ballet, and was himself a dancer of distinction. In 1651, although still a boy of thirteen, he made his debut in the ballet *Cassandre*. At first, with occasional exceptions, the ballets included those representations of human misery, the crippled, the hunchbacked, the maimed, and the palsied, which possessed such a peculiar attraction for the Court; or were they introduced simply to stress the unusual good looks of Louis le Roi Soleil?

Gradually, however, such coarse and crude elements were eliminated, to be replaced by a noble and dignified style, due to the King's refined taste, and the influence of the excellent designers he selected for the adornment of his ballets.

Moreover, the King made two important contributions to the advancement of dancing by establishing the Académie Royale de Danse (1661) and the Académie Royale de Musique (1669). In 1672 a school of dancing was added to the latter and this was the origin of the State ballet. The ballet continued to be a spectacle composed of dancing, painting, music, and singing, but now it passed from restricted performance at Court to the public theatre. The personnel consisted of men alone, the women's roles being taken by youths of feminine build, whose faces were concealed by masks, at this time a fixed part of the dancer's costume.

Rabel was succeeded by Henri Gissey, *Dessinateur ordinaire du Cabinet du Roi*, who designed the costumes for many ballets. But, although all his work is distinguished by an ingenious invention, his masterpiece was the costumes for the celebrated *Carrousel de Louis XIV*, the horse ballet given in front of the Louvre, Paris, in 1662, which has never been surpassed for its splendour. Imagine some five hundred noblemen in magnificent costumes and mounted on gaily caparisoned and beplumed horses, escorted by elaborately dressed attendants.

This glittering troop was divided into five quadrilles, each representing a different nation as interpreted in the fantasy of baroque art, and each having its particular set of colours. First came Romans, in red and gold, led by the King; second, Persians, in brown and red, led by Monsieur; third, Turks, in black and yellow, led by the Prince de Condé; fourth, Indians, in white and gold feathers, led by the Duc d' Enghien; and fifth, Americans, in green and gold, led by the Duc de Guise. This marvellous spectacle, with its figuring and curvetting horses must surely be accounted the apotheosis of the *haute école*.

Gissey died in 1673, when his place was taken by Jean Berain, the greatest of Louis XIV's designers for Court entertainments. Born at Bar le Duc in 1638 he came to Paris in 1659 where he worked as an engraver. In 1671 he was employed by the King and Le Brun in the reproduction of ornaments executed in the Gallery of Apollo under the direction of the First Painter. Soon afterwards he gave up engraving and became a designer, his fertile imagination producing innumerable designs for embroidery, tapestry, wood carvings and the decoration of war vessels. Then, as we have seen, he was appointed to design all costumes and properties required in connection with the festivals and entertainments given by the King.

Berain's costumes for female dancers in the serious or noble style are, in their main features, closely related to contemporary Court dress, the bodice being close-fitting, the skirt following the lines of the hips, to widen slightly as it falls to ankle-level. Sometimes the skirt has a train and a decorative over-skirt, short at the front and long at the back. The sleeves are generally short with falling lace at the elbow. Sometimes the bodice is decorated to suggest scales or armour, sometimes it is decorated with bows and tassels. The head-dress is generally a group of tastefully arranged ostrich plumes set in a cap or helmet, but it may also be a simple *fontange* or lawn cap with wired and goffered front, rising in tiers. The men's costume in the same style follows the now familiar dress *à la romaine*, which at this period shows traces of the influence of Le Brun's paintings of the victories of Alexander the Great. Such, however, are merely the chief characteristics, the artistry of Berain's conceptions lies in their highly decorative quality and the restrained and elegant symbolism introduced into that ornament.

In dresses of a fantastic character, such as marine gods and goddesses, with their suggestion of scaly bodies and the serrated leaves of sea-plants, and head-gear contrived from shells and coral; Furies, with their pendant breasts and straggled locks of twisting serpents; Winds, with their wings and feathers; Follies, with their tinkling bells; Berain's inventive genius finds its fullest flight. This distinction applies no less to those fascinating costumes, at which Gissey, too, was adept, wherein the attributes of a calling are ingeniously combined to form a costume.

To show the extent to which a conventional symbolism in costume design for ballet had become established, and at the same time to make clear its principles, I should like to quote some passages from *Des Ballets Anciens et Modernes* (1681) of Père Ménestrier, which in part describes the ballets of Louis XIV and lays down four conditions regarding costume for ballet.

" The first condition is that the costume should be appropriate to the subject and, if the personages be historical, one should keep as far as possible to the costume of the period. That of the ancient Romans is the most dignified of all, and there is not one that allows the leg more freedom. It is composed of a cuirass with its *lambrequins*. A short mantle accompanies it, reaching half-way down the arms, below which is a pleated silken garment which forms the surcoat. The helmet with an aigrette and plumes is the head-dress which should accompany this dress and, when the dancers represent victorious troops, they must wear garlands of laurels. The same rule applies to foreign nations. Greeks have round caps with a quantity of plumes. The head-dress of the Persians is almost similar. Moors have short and curly hair, their faces black and hands black; they wear no hats, unless they be given fillets sewn with pearls in the form of a diadem. They should wear earrings. Turks and Saracens should be garbed in dolmans and wear turbans with aigrettes. American Indians wear caps with vari-coloured feathers, loin-cloths of the same kind to cover their nakedness, and necklaces of the same feathers of which they carry a bunch in each hand when dancing. Japanese wear large tufts of hair bound at the back . . .

" The second condition is that the costumes should be greatly varied and, if possible, the same kind of dress should not appear twice, or at least the *entrées* should be so devised that there is a long interval between those that are alike. The colour can be changed if it be not possible to make any other difference, as sometimes occurs in historical ballets when all the persons are of the same race and nearly the same station. . . .

" The third condition is that uniformity should be maintained as far as possible in the same *entrées*, that is to say, all those taking part in them should be dressed in the same colour and style if the subject permit.

" The fourth condition is that the costume shall not be cumbersome and shall leave the legs and body quite free to dance. The women's costumes are the least suitable because they must be long.

" If anything be put into the hands of the dancers it should serve for some action. Such as a hammer and trowel with which to imitate building, a sword to mimic fighting ; Rivers pour water out of their urns, Zephyrs make a breeze with bunches of plumes, and the Cyclops strike on an anvil."

Ménestrier then gives general directions for the costuming of familiar characters in ballets :

" The costume of Spring should be green sprinkled with flowers, and a garland of roses. Winter should be dressed in white with a long beard, a furred costume, and appear sluggish in his movements. The dress of Summer should be isabel colour, which is that of the harvest ; she must wear a crown of ears of corn on her head and carry a scythe. That of Autumn should be olive colour or that of dead leaves, with a cornucopia full of fruit, and a garland of vine leaves.

" Winds should be dressed in feathers on account of their lightness ; the Sun in cloth of gold with a gilt head-dress, the Moon in cloth of silver ; both wear a mask, one with golden rays, the other with silver.

" Time should be dressed in four colours denoting the four seasons. For head-dress he should wear a clock-face marking the hours, wings on his back and head, an hour glass in one hand and a scythe in the other. Night should be dressed in black powdered with stars, and wear a crescent moon on her head. Cupid should be dressed in rose-coloured material, covered with flaming hearts, his eyes bandaged, a bow in his hand and a quiver on his back. Hate, on the contrary, should wear a fire-coloured dress and carry a dagger in one hand and poison in the other, or a smoking torch of black wax. The costume should be black because this passion is not free from sadness. Envy should wear a yellow costume dotted with open eyes. Poverty is recognised by a torn dress from which hang parti-coloured rags."

The Arts and Sciences were represented by working patterns of the instruments and signs associated with them into the usual jacket and breeches in the case of the male dancer, or tight bodice and skirt in the case of a female dancer.

In his first years as *Dessinateur du Roi,* Berain appears to have confined his attention to costumes, but, in 1681, he was responsible for both dresses and scenery of the ballet *Le Triomphe de l'Amour*, produced at Saint-Germain, at which the composer, Lully, introduced female dancers for the first time. The ladies of the Court took part, the Princesse de Conti and Mlle. de Nantes being among the first *danseuses*. A little later the ballet was given publicly at Paris, when the Académie de Musique furnished four *danseuses*, of whom Mlle. Lafontaine was the leader and who consequently became the first *première danseuse*. From then onwards Berain was responsible for all the settings of the opera-ballets subsequently composed by Lully.

Jean Berain died in 1711 and was succeeded as *Dessinateur du Cabinet du Roi* by his son, also named Jean, who held this office until roughly 1721. Little is known of his activities beyond the fact that his work showed the influence of his father.

Berain the younger was followed by Claude Gillot, in whose studio both Watteau and Lancret worked in the days of their youth. As a designer for the ballet, Gillot is best remembered for his costumes for *Les Eléments*, presented at the Tuileries on New Year's Eve, 1721, which have been preserved in a series of 84 engravings by his pupil, Joullain. Something of the Berain manner is retained, but the stiff brocades dear to that artist are replaced by soft materials. The first thing that strikes one about Gillot's costumes is their comparative simplicity. But although they are not without charm, they lack the nobility of Berain's conceptions. Two important innovations, however, are to be observed : the fuller, bell-shaped skirt, resulting from the introduction, in 1718, of *paniers*, which soon became very fashionable, and, in the case of the male dancers, the short, hooped, kilt-like skirt, known as a *tonnelet* (little cask), which henceforth is typical for the greater part of the century of male dancers in the noble style.

From 1744 to 1748 the principle designer to the Opera was François Boucher, who devised a number of settings and costumes for lyric dramas but, apparently, few for Ballet. It is said that he was not enamoured of his task and resigned his post.

Boucher was succeeded by Jean Baptiste Martin, something of whose brilliance may be gleaned from an examination of the collection of twenty of his designs in colour, variously engraved by Martin and Gaillard, which was published by the author about 1763. In these lovely drawings we see the conventional attributes of the personages of classical mythology, and those " Indians," " Mexicans," " Africans," " Incas," and other exotic races dear to the ballet-masters of the eighteenth century, resolved with rare taste and feeling for design into the most elegant and superb costumes. Martin is Berain's only peer.

Martin was followed in 1760 by Louis Boquet who retained office until 1782. Boquet's designs with their doll-like faces and tiny heads, waists, hands, and feet, and, by way of contrast, their large skirts, appear the embodiment of sophistication. The costumes imitated the prevailing mode and were adorned with garlands of chiffon, lace, ostrich-feather tips, or artificial flowers. The skirt followed the course of fashion in that it passed from a round to an oval shape and then grew larger and flatter until the advent of the French Revolution; the buskins gave place to the shoes and stockings of the period. The perukes and costumes were in general much more exaggerated in the time of Louis XV than in the days of the preceding monarch; on the other hand the actual decoration of the costume was simpler.

Another type of costume was that worn by the *danseur comique* or character dancer. It was a fanciful version of peasant dress trimmed with a profusion of ribbon.

At least three notable attempts at reform of the dancer's costume took place during the reign of Louis XV. Camargo introduced the *entrechat* in 1730. Although this step had previously been done by men, it had not hitherto been achieved by a woman. But, to gain greater freedom for her legs, Camargo caused her dress to be shortened by several inches, thus permitting the calf to be seen. Camargo, moreover, had the forethought to wear a small pair of close-fitting knickers while executing her new *temps d'élévation*, a tremendous innovation if it be recalled that knickers did not come into general wear, at any rate in England, until the eighteen-forties. It seems not unreasonable to assume that this intimate garment was the origin of the later *maillot* or tights, so that it is no exaggeration to state that the evolution of that article of dress permitted as great a change in the art of dancing as did the invention of gunpowder on warfare.

That Camargo's precaution was justified is proved by the mishap that happened to a young *danseuse* called Mariette who, while springing into the air during the execution of a *pas*, caught her dress on a piece of scenery with the most embarrassing results to the wearer. Soon afterwards the police authorities issued an order requiring all actresses to wear *caleçons de précaution* before appearing on the stage.

In 1734, Camargo's rival, Marie Sallé, danced at London on February 14th, in *Pygmalion*, a ballet of her own composition, in which she appeared " without paniers, petticoat, and bodice, her hair loose and without any ornament on her head: she was dressed only in a single muslin robe which was draped about her in the manner of a Greek statue."

Finally, in 1760, the celebrated *maître de ballet*, Jean Georges Noverre, published his now famous *Lettres sur la Danse et les Ballets* in which he condemned the dancer's costumes in general and masks in particular. It is of interest to cite some passages from his book since no work before or since has produced so great an influence for good in the matter of ballet presentation.

" Let us pass to costume; its variety and accuracy are as rare as in music, in ballets and in simple dancing. Obstinacy in adhering to out-worn tradition is the same in every part of opera, it is the monarch of all it surveys. Greek, Roman, Shepherd, Hunter, Warrior, Faun, Forester, Games, Pleasures, Laughs, Tritons, Winds, Fires, Dreams, High Priests, Celebrants—all these characters are cut to the same pattern and differ only in the colour and ornaments with which a desire for ostentatious display rather than good taste has caused them to be bespattered at caprice. Tinsel glitters everywhere; Peasant, Sailor, Hero—all are covered alike. The more a costume is decorated with gew-gaws, spangles, gauze and net, the greater the admiration it procures the ignorant spectator.

" I would do away with those *tonnelets* which in certain dancing positions transport, as it were, the hip to the shoulder and conceal all the contours of the body. I would banish all uniformity in costume, an indifferent, ungraceful device which owes its origin to lack of taste. I should prefer light and simple draperies of contrasting colours worn in such a manner as to reveal the dancer's figure . . . . I desire beautiful folds, fine masses with the ends fluttering and producing ever-changing forms as the dance becomes more and more animated; everything should convey a sense of filminess.

" I would reduce by three-quarters the ridiculous *paniers* of our *danseuses*, they are equally opposed to the freedom, speed, prompt and lively action of the dance. Again they deprive the figure of the elegance and correct proportions which it should have; they lessen the charms of the arms; they impede and trouble the *danseuse* to such a degree that the movement of her *panier* generally takes up far more of her attention than that of her arms and legs.

" Physiognomy, then, is that part of us most necessary

to expression; well, why conceal it on the stage by a mask and prefer a clumsy art to beautiful nature? How can the dancer paint if he be deprived of his most essential colours? How can he transfer to the breast of the spectator the passions which consume his own, if he himself remove the means and cover his face with a piece of cardboard which ever appears sad and uniform, cold and motionless?

"Can the passions be revealed and break through the screen which the dancer places between the spectator and himself? Can he make a single one of those artificial faces express the innumerable characteristics of the different passions? Will it be possible for him to change the form which the mould has given to the mask? Because a mask of whatever kind is either cold or pleasing, serious or comic, sad or grotesque. The modeller affords it but one permanent and unvarying character."

The mask was abolished in 1772 as the result of an incident during the revival of Rameau's opera, *Castor et Pollux*. Gaetano Vestris, as usual, should have danced the *entrée* of Apollo in the fifth act. As this character he appeared in an enormous peruke, his features covered by a mask, and wore on his breast a large sun of gilded copper. But on this occasion Vestris was unable to appear and his part was allotted to Maximilien Gardel, a well-known dancer of the period and pupil of Noverre, who consented to appear provided he was permitted to discard both wig and mask. The public was pleased and henceforth the solo dancers abandoned the mask. It was, however, worn for some time longer by the *corps de ballet* for the representation of Shades, Winds, and Furies. Even as late as 1785 the Winds wore the usual mask with puffed-out cheeks, but no longer carried the symbolic pair of bellows.

This juncture affords an appropriate opportunity to pause in our examination of costume and consider the development of stage decoration throughout the latter half of the seventeenth and the whole of the eighteenth centuries. As a general comment it may be stated that Italian designers inspired or planned the settings for the principal theatres in most European capitals. The basic settings consisted of flat one-sided wings set parallel to the proscenium frame and running in grooves, and arranged to provide a dozen changes or more. With the development of machinery, the wings could also be raised to the "flies." The final scene was generally a backcloth painted in perspective. The settings were mainly architectural—temples, palaces, or gardens—suited to the classic themes common to ballets and operas at this period.

A very important Italian designer of this period was Lodovico Burnacini (1634-1707), celebrated for the extraordinary fantasy and splendour of the baroque costumes and settings he created for the entertainments presented at the Court of the Emperor Leopold I of Austria.

The principal scenic artist at the Court of Louis XIV was Giacomo Torelli da Fano (1608-78), something of whose work has been preserved in a series of engravings. His scenes are largely simple studies in perspective, sometimes almost crude and sometimes so delicately and so imaginatively conceived as to seem the realisation of a poet's fantasy. His cloud scenes are superb. Yet he was not only a designer but also an engineer of rare ability, a faculty which enabled him to achieve such stupendous stage illusions that more than one of his contemporaries suspected him of being in league with the Devil.

In 1660, Torelli retired and was succeeded by Gaspare Vigarani (1586-1663), another expert engineer who, from sheer envy, destroyed his predecessor's machines. Vigarani was responsible for the construction at the Tuileries of the great *Salle des Machines* where, on a stage 31 feet wide and four times as deep, the most spectacular effects were achieved.

Vigarani was followed by Giovanni Servandoni (1695-1766), who did not follow the usual practice of making his columns diminish in height according to their distance from the spectator, but allowed them to vanish into the "flies," to infinity, as it were. He also shifted the angle of vision from the conventional central viewpoint, thus achieving novel effects in perspective which he heightened by using groups of dancers graduated according to height, and sometimes introducing in that part of the scene farthest from the audience children dressed as adults.

But, important as were the contributions of these designers, they were over-shadowed by that great dynasty of scenic artists known as the Bibienas, whose name is derived from the birthplace of the head of the family. The founder was Giovanni Maria Galli (1619-65), the succession passing in turn to his sons, Ferdinando (1657-1743) and Francesco (1659-1739), his grandsons, Antonio (1700-1776) and Guiseppe (1696-1751), and his great-grandsons, Alessandro and Carlo.

All practised their art in Italy with the exception of Alessandro and Carlo who worked in Germany and Russia respectively. In the settings of the Bibienas the art of stage perspective is seen *in excelsis*; no other stage designs at any period have equalled their work in grandeur and nobility of conception. Another important designer was Gian Piranesi (1720-78) who, although following the school of the Bibienas, invested his settings with a novel sense of drama by bold contrasts of light and shade. There is still one more designer to be mentioned—Pietro Gonzago (died in 1831), who designed so many settings for the operas and ballets produced at the Imperial Russian Theatres.

But to return to costume. The French Revolution which ushered in the fashion for light dresses, modelled on the classic tunics and robes of the ancient Greek and Roman republics, caused high-heeled shoes to be replaced by heelless shoes tied sandal-wise up the leg; the toes were pointed. These fashions were soon transferred to the stage as can be seen in certain prints of Maria Medina Viganò, a celebrated dancer of the period, and in some of the engravings which accompany the *Traité Elémentaire, Théorique et Pratique de l'Art de la Danse* of Carlo Blasis (Milan, 1820).

In 1791 there was another important innovation in the costume of the male dancer and destined to exercise considerable influence on the development of his technique. This event is associated with the opera *Corisandre*, by de Linières and Le Bailly, presented at the Opéra on March 8th, when, in one of the dances, Didelot, in the role of Zephyr, appeared in a transparent tunic.

The shortening of the dress and the use of transparent material in its construction led to the introduction of *maillot* or tights, a combination of long stockings with skin-tight knickers. The invention of this garment is usually attributed to Maillot—hence the name—a costumier at the Opéra at the beginning of the century. But the use of tights was certainly known to Guimard, who retired in 1790; moreover, the transparent dresses associated with the Merveilleuses must have necessitated the wearing of a similar garment.

During the early eighteen-twenties, there were three distinct types of dancers: the serious or noble style; the *demi-caractère*; and the *caractère*—these terms indicating the style of dancing—each having a basically characteristic costume.

The male dancer in the serious style wore a Greek *chiton* of light material, his legs were bare and his feet shod with sandals strapped round the ankle and base of the calf. The *danseuse* was dressed in a filmy robe—sometimes damped to cling to the figure and more clearly reveal its lines—ending midway between the ankle and calf; the feet were encased in buskins.

The male dancer in the *demi-caractère* style wore doublet, trunks, and long hose, evidently inspired by Renaissance fashions, and a flat-brimmed cap adorned with an ostrich feather. Whether this dress was suggested by certain of the costumes designed by Isabey for the Coronation of Napoleon I, or whether it was selected as being a costume at once decorative and allowing full play for movement, I cannot say. The *danseuse* wore a theatricalised version of the cylindrical low-necked dress, gathered beneath the breasts, which remained in general use until 1821, but continued to be seen on the stage in ballets for some years later.

The male dancer in the *caractère* style wore a theatricalised version of the open-necked shirt, short coat, and breeches common to village youths, while the *danseuse* wore a similar version of the dress of a contemporary village girl.

Two designers of particular interest must be mentioned in connection with the first quarter of the nineteenth century. They are Auguste Garnerey and Hippolyte Lecomte.

Garnerey was a fashionable artist, at one time drawing-master to Queen Hortense, and a friend of the Duchesse de Berry, to whose influence he owed his appointment as designer to the Opéra, which post he retained until his death in 1824. His designs are most attractive and reveal considerable ingenuity in adapting contemporary dress to suggest the several lands and periods of the ballets to be presented. One of his characteristics is a partiality for jewelled embroideries, which he uses with great taste as a means of decoration. In the Bibliothèque de l'Opéra, Paris, there are preserved a number of his pen-and-ink sketches, which are particularly interesting for their marginal notes. But for an idea of their colour we must rely on the lithographs of Engelmann after Garnerey.

Hippolyte Lecomte was originally a painter of historical episodes, and, as might be expected, accuracy rather than fantasy is the distinguishing quality of his workmanlike drawings. He was designer to the Opéra from 1825 to 1830 and his chief interest as a creator of costumes for ballets resides in his adaptations of national costume, for instance, those for the Tyrolean dancers in Rossini's *Guillaume Tell* (1829), and his Oriental costumes, such as those for *Le Dieu et la Bayadère*, (1830).

During the Restoration, the chaste Vicomte Sosthènes de la Rochefoucauld, Superintendent of the Royal Theatres, caused the dancers' skirts to be lengthened and ordered them to wear long pantaloons reaching below the skirt in place of tights. Happily this ridiculous concession to modesty did not long endure. During this same period (about 1830), the heelless shoe became square-toed.

A decade or more earlier, *pointes* came into use, for there is a lithograph (dated 1821) by F. Waldeck of Fanny Bias as Flora in *Flore et Zéphyre*, in which the dancer is represented *sur les pointes*. There is a later and better known lithograph after a drawing by A. E. Chalon (dated 1831) of Marie Taglioni as Flora in the same ballet (revived London, 1830), in which she is shown poised *sur la pointe*. Note that in both instances the toe of the shoe is unblocked, being merely stiffened by darning. But it is difficult to establish the exact date of the introduction of *pointes*, or to state which dancer first achieved this position.

In 1832, when the influence of the Romantic Period was to be seen for the first time in Ballet, the familiar skirt of muslin or tarlatan came into being. It is regarded as the creation of the painter, Eugène Lami, for Taglioni's costume in the title-role of *La Sylphide*, first produced in March of that year. The bodice is tight-fitting, leaving the neck and shoulders bare, the sleeves are wide and very short, the skirt is bell-shaped and ends half-way between the ankle and the knee. The costume is white, relieved only by a garland of flowers placed on the head, a pearl bracelet on each wrist, and a simple pearl necklace.

It is a strange fact, however, that although Lami's designs for the costumes for *La Sylphide* are preserved in the Bibliothèque de l'Opéra, the most important design of all, that for the Sylphide, is not to be found. Yet that ethereal costume[1], planned to envelop the dancer in a milky haze from which her face and limbs now and again emerged like those of an embodied spirit, has all the characteristics of Lami's delicate pencil. Or can it be that Taglioni herself conceived the costume unaided or in collaboration with Lami? But while a doubt may still linger as to who should receive credit for the creation of the dress for the Sylphide, there can be no question as to the costume's overwhelming success, for henceforth the muslin skirt became the accepted costume, one might almost say, uniform of the dancer of the classical ballet.

This fact established, it is of interest to note that whereas, previous to the production of *La Sylphide*, ballet costume was very largely a theatricalised version of contemporary dress,

the Sylphide costume, with occasional exceptions, remains the accepted costume for the *danseuse* of the classical ballet. Certainly there have been variations in the length of the sleeve, the shape of the yoke, the style of decoration, and the length of the skirt, but in its main details the costume has continued unchanged. In the last third of the nineteenth century ballet-shoes were blocked to give additional support to the toes, but it is difficult to ascertain precisely when or by whom the innovation was introduced. It can be stated, however, that the shoes worn by the *ballerina*, Emma Livry, at the time of her fatal accident in 1862, were unblocked.

Resuming our examination of the costume proper, it should be noted that by the eighteen-forties the short sleeves became little more than shoulder-straps, which in the 'eighties were adorned with flares of muslin. The skirt was made shorter and fuller, and stuffed with additional muslin petticoats until it became shaped like a lampshade. With the development of technique and the constant striving towards the achievement of more and more difficult, almost acrobatic, *tours de force*, the skirt, in order to afford the legs the necessary freedom, became shorter and shorter, until it resembled a powder-puff.

In the eighteen-thirties the white ballet skirt was primarily associated with the supernatural beings typical of the Romantic Ballet—sylphides, naiads, sprites, and incarnations of butterflies and flowers, and was decorated with wings, sea-plants, coral, stars, and similar attributes to suggest the character's natural domain.

But there were two sides to the Romantic Ballet, not only the region of legend and the mystic realm of sprites, but the world of realism, which latter inspired such ballets as *Esmeralda*, *Catarina*, and *Paquita*, which are set respectively in Paris of the Middle Ages, the Abruzzi, and Spain during the French invasion. In this type of ballet the dress had to suggest both period and nationality. So, the ghost-like ballet-skirt would be adapted to suggest, say, a Spanish girl, by making the bodice red and the skirt yellow, adorned with black lace. If the costume were to be Polish, then the dress might be pale blue, with the bodice, sleeves, and skirt tipped with white fur. Even the Japanese kimono, as in Hansen's *Le Rêve* (1890), was adapted to the ballet skirt.

[1] It is shown in many paintings and lithographs of the period.

Once the convention was grasped it was not difficult for the public to recognise the dancer's assumed nationality. Ribbon of varied materials, widths, and hues played a great part in the decoration of bodice and skirt; sometimes it was set in wide vertical lines on the skirt, sometimes in groups of narrow vertical lines, sometimes it ran horizontally along the dress in one, two, or more tiers. The use of ribbon as a basis of decoration could provide the subject for an essay in itself. But towards the end of the nineteenth century, decorative design, as applied to ballet costume, steadily deteriorated and sometimes produced results which were frankly hideous.

But while the main features of the dancer's costume were established, the dancer's *coiffure* followed the prevailing fashion, whatever character she interpreted, and it was the rule rather than the exception for the *ballerina* to wear a diamond crescent or tiara. Ballet-goers saw nothing incongruous in the dancer's representing a simple peasant with her hair elaborately dressed and wearing jewelled bracelets and necklaces in the most fashionable style. Another curious anomaly was that although the dancers, from *corps de ballet* to *danseuse étoile*, usually wore the traditional ballet skirt, the supers were dressed in more or less correct costumes of the period of the ballet. These conditions may be said to have been in force in the ballet companies of all European countries in the second half of the nineteenth century.

The costume for the male dancer in classical ballet has continued to consist of tights, shorts, and doublet or jerkin, with such variations and adaptations as might be offered by the period and place of action of the ballet. But Taglioni's triumph in *La Sylphide* and the victories gained by her great contemporaries—Fanny Elssler, Carlotta Grisi, Lucile Grahn, and Fanny Cerito—led to the decline and eventual eclipse of the male dancer who became little more than a *porteur*, while in some instances, in France and England, he was actually replaced by a female dancer dressed to represent a man. This led to another convention which has to be accepted in good faith, since the rounded curves of the female form at this period could hardly be mistaken for the figure of a man. The Imperial Russian Ballet, however, with its splendid *corps* of male dancers, never made use of the travesty dancer[1]. In 1881 Enrico Cecchetti's appearance at His Majesty's Theatre in Manzotti's *Excelsior* did much to restore the male dancer to respect; the

process was completed by the successive London appearances of Mordkin, Nijinsky, and other notable Russian dancers.

The influence of *La Sylphide* on ballet costume was no less potent on settings for ballet. After *La Sylphide*, as Gautier remarks, "the twelve palaces in marble and gold of the Olympians were relegated to the dust of the store-rooms, and the scene-painters received orders only for romantic forests and valleys, illumined by the pretty German moonlight of Heinrich Heine's ballads."

No doubt such effects were enhanced by the application of the devices which the Alsatian artist, de Loutherbourg (1735-1812), devised for David Garrick's productions at Drury Lane, for John O'Keefe credits him with the invention of "transparent scenery—moonshine, sunshine, fire, volcanoes, etc.—as also breaking the scene into several pieces by the laws of perspective, showing miles and miles distance." Moreover, candles, which had so long remained the principal source of illumination, were replaced in 1822 by gas, which, easy of control, produced a soft mellow light of great charm and, unlike candles, capable of being intensified or dimmed at will in whole or in part.

Pierre Ciceri (1782-1868) was the chief designer of settings to the Opera from 1815 to 1847 and devised one or more scenes for over 300 productions, including several important ballets such as *Cendrillon*, *La Belle au Bois Dormant*, *La Sylphide*, and *Giselle*. Among other designers for ballet settings at the Opera from 1832 to 1890 mention must be made of Feuchères, Dieterle, Despléchin, Philastre, Cambon, Séchan, Rubé, Thierry, Nolau, Chaperon, Lavastre, and Daran.

At this point I should like to resume the discussion of costume. Lecomte was replaced in 1831 by one of his pupils, a young artist called Paul Lormier, who held office until 1887. In 1855 he was appointed *Chef de l'Habillement* and was accorded an assistant in the person of Alfred Albert. Lormier began his apprenticeship under Lami, whom he helped with the costumes for the ballet in the fifth act of Auber's famous opera, *Gustave III* (1832). Both Lormier and Albert were conscientious workers who took great pains to study the dress of the period of the ballet or opera in preparation before designing their own costumes, but they were competent rather than inspired. There were other artists

[1] In *La Fille Mal Gardée*, however, the character role of Mother Simone was invariably taken by a male dancer dressed as a woman.

who from time to time contributed designs for ballet costume, but there is no space to do more than mention their names—Henri d'Orchevillers, Marilhat, Lacoste, and Bianchini.

Parisian successes such as *La Sylphide* and *Giselle* were soon reproduced in London, generally with new scenery painted for the occasion. Again, many of Perrot's best ballets had their first performance in London and for those, too, special scenery had to be designed and painted. The artist responsible for many of these sets was William Grieve (1800-44)[1], who was scene-painter (which at this time also meant designer) to Drury Lane and Her Majesty's Theatres. He was particularly noted for his moonlit scenes. In this connection it may be of interest to reproduce a contemporary impression of the lighting preparatory to Cerito's execution of her famous *Pas de l'Ombre* in Perrot's *Ondine*. "The mountains in the background which shine with the light of day, become red with the tints of sunset, and at last the moon rises, and a full blue light is thrown upon the stage."[2]

After Grieve, the settings for ballet in London, like those in foreign capitals, strayed further and further from the theatre and became more and more representational. No longer was the ideal to suggest, but to imitate, to achieve a coloured photograph. Many of the scenes were elaborate built-up sets carried out with an almost incredible passion for detail.

In Italy, the Scala at Milan became the centre of the spectacular and propagandist ballets inaugurated by Luigi Manzotti with his *Excelsior* (1881), *Amor* (1886), and *Sport* (1897), which were not ballets in the present understanding of the term, but mimed episodes varied with danced *ensembles* and stupendous processions of supers, often accompanied by horses and elephants. Manzotti's principal designer was Alfredo Edel, whose costumes were pretty-pretty, fanciful versions of contemporary or historical dress. Animals, vegetables, insects, flowers, birds, reptiles, jewels—there was nothing which the ingenious designer could not translate into terms of costume for ballet.

Manzotti's *Excelsior* was reproduced in London and no doubt inspired the type of ballet—a combination of extravaganza, spectacle, and revue, with dancing—which was associated with the Alhambra and the Empire Theatres from 1878 to 1911 and from 1887 to 1914 respectively.

Most of the costumes for the Alhambra ballets were designed by or executed under the supervision of M. Alias (some of his dresses were the work of Comelli), who supplied every costume for every production at that theatre for well over a quarter of a century.

The costumes for the Empire ballets were designed from 1887 by C. Wilhelm, who also wrote the themes of many of their most successful ballets. His costumes were superior in design and conception to those of Alias, and showed a keen sense of theatrical effect, but they were of the pretty-pretty type then fashionable.

In the Imperial Russian Ballet there was the same passion for spectacular setting throughout all the second half of the nineteenth century when the company was ruled by Marius Petipa. " A magnificent garden," " a splendid palace," " a public square," " a throne room "—are directions to the scene-painter which appear with almost monotonous regularity in the *scenarii* of ballets. The scene-designer at this period was a craftsman rather than an artist. He had a comprehensive knowledge of historic ornament and the several styles of architecture, but his chief aim was to achieve richness and spaciousness, and with adroit managing of perspective to suggest effects of distance. The scene-designer's work, then, was in general undistinguished.

As the reader considers the above paragraphs concerning the nineteenth century he will observe another curious fact, namely, that hardly ever were both setting and costumes entrusted to one designer.

Let us leave the Ballet for a moment and glance at stage decoration generally. Here, too, in the matter of setting, naturalism was the prime objective. The first reaction occurred about 1890 and was instituted by a group of writers and artists termed *Symbolistes*, who were led by Paul Fort. They demanded the simplification of stage decoration, the abolition of the perspective back-cloth, and insisted on the harmonious coordination of costume and setting, which must express the style-atmosphere of the play.

In Russia, a few years later, a similar contest was waged between realism in production—carried to the farthest extent in the Moscow Art Theatre, directed by Stanislavsky—and a new movement in the theatre sponsored by S. Mamontov, a rich Moscow manufacturer.

[1] Grieve was a member of the celebrated family of scene-designers, founded by John Henderson Grieve (1770-1845). He had two sons, William, mentioned above, and Thomas, who designed the settings at Covent Garden Theatre, first for the Kembles, then Laporte, and later for Mr. & Mrs. Charles Mathews. Thomas had a son, Thomas Walford, who was also a scene-designer.
[2] *The Times*, January 23rd., 1843.

Stanislavsky devoted his attention to the Drama; Mamontov's interest was centred on Opera, for the production of which he built himself a special theatre.

Mamontov was one of the great pioneers in securing recognition for Russian music, but his principal interest in relation to the subject of this introduction, is that he was perhaps the first person in Russia to form the conclusion that a stage setting could be something much more than a background for the actor or singer. He felt that scenery could be used to provide a beautiful picture, to evoke a fitting sense of style-atmosphere; and he was the first director to employ genuine artists such as Vasnetzov and Korovine to design the settings for his productions.

In 1899 Mamontov founded an art journal entitled *Mir Iskusstva* (*The World of Art*) This venture was another step forward in the campaign against naturalism. The journal was edited by Serge Diaghilev, whose staff and contributors included Alexandre Benois, Bakst, Korovine, Serov, and other fine artists. These painters, although not professional designers for the stage, had an intense love for the theatre, which led them actively to promote the reform of stage decoration, not only by championing the cause in their journal, but by actual work in the theatre secured to some extent through Diaghilev's influence.

On July 22nd of the same year Prince Serge Wolkonsky was appointed director of the Imperial Theatres. He commissioned Golovine and Korovine to design settings for the ballets: *Le Lac des Cygnes*, *Don Quichotte*, and *Le Miroir Magique*. He also attached Diaghilev to the directorate as an official for special missions and, when it was decided to revive Delibes's *Sylvia*, entrusted him with the artistic direction of the ballet. It was to have had settings and costumes by a combined group of artists—Benois, Bakst, Korovine, Lanceray, and Serov. Unfortunately, Diaghilev quarrelled with Prince Wolkonsky and resigned. Soon afterwards the director resigned owing to a difference with Kshesinskaya, the *prima ballerina assoluta*.

Wolkonsky was succeeded by Teliakovsky, who also gave opportunities to rising young painters, including Bakst, who, in 1902, made his debut as stage designer with his setting for a version of Euripides's *Hippolytus*, and was next commissioned to design the setting and costumes for *Puppen-Fée*, an old German ballet which, when revived by Diaghilev some seventeen years later and provided with new choreography by

Massine, was to become famous as *La Boutique Fantasque*.

About 1904 a new apostle of the dance appeared in the person of the American dancer, Isadora Duncan. She condemned the traditional costume of the ballet, observing that one did not play the piano with gloved hands, and hence the first essential for the liberation of the dance was to free the dancer from her short skirt, tight bodice, pink tights, and satin shoes.

At this same period a young Russian choreographer, Michel Fokine, was consumed with a like desire to reform ballet costume and rescue it from the confusion of periods and styles, but, contrary to Duncan, he did not wish to destroy anything. He wanted Greek costumes, bare feet, and flowing tresses for Greek ballets; the traditional ballet skirt and tights for romantic ballets; heeled shoes and Spanish costume for Spanish ballets; Russian costumes for Russian ballets; and so on.

In 1906, Diaghilev began his crusade of showing Russian art to Western Europe, as represented by Paris. He opened his campaign with an exhibition of painting of both the classical and modern schools, which was followed by a series of concerts of Russian music (1907), presentations of Russian opera (1908), and, finally, performances of Russian ballet, as interpreted in the new school founded by Michel Fokine (1909).

It is important to record that, in one of his early ballets, *Eunice* (1907), Fokine made the bold venture of dressing his dancers in Greek *chitons*, but, since, at this period, the use of bare legs and feet on the stage would have been considered indecent, he compromised by letting his dancers wear tights with the feet painted to suggest toes. The next year, Fokine produced *Une Nuit d'Egypte*, later known as *Cléopâtre*. This ballet had been prepared for Petipa, who for some reason never carried it out, notwithstanding that the costumes had already been made. The women's dresses of the conventional type, consisted of tights and ballet-skirt adorned with an Egyptian decorative motif. Fokine rejected those costumes and devised new ones out of close-fitting smocks, bound about the waist with a sash. He also contrived Egyptian head-dresses from twisted tow and designed a special make-up by which means the eyes were lengthened; finally, the dancers' bodies were darkened with a little brown, an unprecedented innovation at this period. In the course of time, by a succession of such reforms and with the aid of genuine artists like Bakst, Benois, Golovine, and Korovine, he saw many of his ideals brought to realisation.

The ballets chosen by Diaghilev for his first season of ballet in Western Europe had settings and costumes variously designed by Benois, Bakst, and Roehrich, whose colours and compositions radiated beauty. They were successful attempts to evoke a mood, a place, or a period in terms of colour and design.

If the reader will examine specimens of the work of these three painters of that period, it will be observed that the old theories of naturalism and perspective are rejected. There are no longer gigantic interiors and landscapes, laboriously constructed to resemble as nearly as possible the actual things; on the contrary, the scenes suggest large-scale water-colours in which harmoniously clad figures dance and mime.

This double revelation of new thought in ballet production and the new school of stage decoration made an extraordinary impression on the spectators, particularly on those who practised the arts. Ballet, which had begun to grow jaded and seemingly incapable of further progress, was offered a new and unsuspected world of endeavour. There can be no doubt that the new stage decoration promoted a revolution in scenic art, whose influence still endures.

It is of interest to examine briefly the qualities of those painters who contributed so much to the success of Diaghilev's first season of ballet.

Benois's art is distinguished by a particular sense of aristocratic refinement; he has the fantasy of Berain allied to the delicate colour sense of Boquet, and is seen at his best in designs associated with the eighteenth century, a period for which he has a particular regard.

Roehrich's work has a rugged primitiveness, at once savage and grandiose, which makes him an ideal designer for the evocation of early times.

Bakst was a master of the difficult art of blending colour, and he arranged his palette as a composer selects his key. In his hands colour could be as potent as a drug. Pink cloys, one shade of green soothes, another jars, one tone of red maddens, black and white depress, white purifies and chills—so Bakst played on the spectator's senses to induce a mood in harmony with the ballet. He could be romantic as in *Le Carnaval*; sensuous, almost erotic as in *Schéhérazade*; mystical, as in *Le Dieu Bleu*; barbaric, as in *Thamar*; lyrical as in *Narcisse*.

Of all the artists I have mentioned, Bakst exerted the greatest influence on the design of his day. His settings and costumes, with their revelation of the immense possibilities of colour and form, were acclaimed, seized upon, and imitated the world over. At one time his name was on everyone's lips. In recent years there has been a tendency on the part of some writers to regard his work as a little crude, even a shade vulgar. It is a not uncommon failing for the pupil to borrow from the master, and then decry his benefactor. There are several designers who might never have come to flower but for the influence of Léon Bakst.

He had great originality and a wonderful sense of the theatre; notice, too, how often his designs show not a lay figure on which clothes have been super-imposed, but a figure in the very act of movement, so that the effect of a costume during an actual dance can be calculated to some purpose. Yet, with all his own gifts, Bakst did not neglect to study the designers of days gone by, and now and again the student will remark a trace of Berain, Martin, or the Bibienas, for example, never copied, but used as a means of inspiration for a conception of his own, or transmuted by his own genius.

Russian painters—with the single exception of J. M. Sert—continued to provide the settings for the Diaghilev Company until 1917, and there were several additions to the original group, for instance, Dobuzhinsky, Goncharova, and Larionov. The colour note was continually heightened to reach its peak with Goncharova's setting for *Le Coq d'Or* (1914), in which certain scenes, conceived in the spirit of decoration of early Russian chapbooks, were overwhelming in their effect. This purely Russian form of decoration was continued with great success by Larionov in *The Midnight Sun* (1915), *Contes Russes* (1917), and finally in *Chout* (1921), but, in the last-named work, the colour contrast was too strident and inclined to reduce the choreography to a subordinate position.

From 1917 onwards, with a few exceptions, Diaghilev selected his designers from modernist painters of easel pictures such as Derain, Matisse, Laurencin, Braque, Gris, Bauchant, and Rouault; or from advance-guard artists like Picasso, Ernst, Miro, Gabo, Pevsner, Tchelichev, and Di Chirico. There was that one final orgy of colour in *Chout* and then the vivid hues of the Russian decorators gave place to the pale, clear tints inaugurated by Picasso, slowly to descend the colour scale until they reached the whites and greys of the costumes in *Ode*.

There were many excellent settings achieved

during this period, such as Bakst's evocation of Longhi and Guardi in *The Good Humoured Ladies*; Derain's *Boutique Fantasque*; Picasso's settings for *Le Tricorne* and *Pulcinella*; Bakst's essay in the grand manner, *The Sleeping Princess*, which recalled the Bibienas; Laurencin's *Les Biches*; and Pruna's *Les Matelots*.

The second decade of the Diaghilev Company was rich in experiment, for it included *Parade*, the first ballet to have a cubist setting, which was designed by Picasso; *Noces*, with its bleak and sombre setting by Gontcharova; three ballets with constructivist settings, *Le Pas d'Acier*, *La Chatte*, and *Ode*; and *Le Bal*, in which Di Chirico made use of architectural motifs in both setting and costumes.

But the Diaghilev organisation was not the only company to contribute to the advancement of stage decoration. In 1920 another troupe, known as the Ballets Suédois, was formed by Rolf de Maré; this company consisted of Swedish and Danish dancers with Jean Borlin, a Swede, for choreographer.

This company endured for five years, during which period twenty-two ballets were produced and shown to the principal cities of Europe and America. Many of those ballets were presented with an artistry of stage decoration equal to those of the better-known Diaghilev company.

The first productions of the *Ballets Suédois* were decorated by Swedish painters such as Nils Dardel and Einar Nerman. Gradually, however, in the director's attempt to discover new paths for the development of ballet, the most modernist painters were commissioned to design settings, some of which mark a definite stage in the decoration of ballet. Take, for instance, *Skating Rink* and *La Création du Monde*, both designed by the cubist painter, Fernand Léger; then the unusual setting by Andrée Parr for Claudel's philosophic ballet, *L'Homme et son Désir*; and the very advanced *Relâche*, with setting by Picabia. This last was more iconoclastic even than anything attempted by Diaghilev.

Diaghilev died in 1929 and his troupe was disbanded. Towards 1932 the nucleus of a new company began to form at Monte Carlo under the joint management of Col. W. de Basil and René Blum. This troupe was known as *Les Ballets Russes de Monte Carlo*. Later the directors parted and two companies were formed, respectively known as *Les Ballets Russes de Col. de Basil* and *Les Ballets de Monte Carlo*, the latter directed by René Blum.

The first of these two companies acquired a number of the Diaghilev ballets which were revived with the original settings, or others based on the original productions, and, in addition, many new ballets were produced for which the following painters contributed designs: Cecil Beaton, the Comte E. de Beaumont, Christian Bérard, Raoul Dufy, André Derain, Alice Halicka, Jean Hugo, Albert Johnson, Eugène Lourie, André Masson, Oliver Messel, Joan Miro, Pierre Roy, Irene Sharaff, and Constantine Terechkovich. One of the most successful was Miro's *surréaliste* setting for *Jeux d'Enfants*.

In 1938 de Basil relinquished the direction of the company bearing his name which, under new management, was styled *Educational Ballets*. In 1939 de Basil again became director, and, when the company arrived in New York early in 1940, preparatory to an American season, its title was changed to the *Original Ballet Russe*. During these two periods new ballets were produced with designs by A. Benois, G. di Chirico, Christo Fanetti, N. Goncharova, K. & F. Martin, and Sergey Sudeikine.

M. Blum had the artistic collaboration of M. Dobuzhinsky for his revival of *Coppelia*, of Derain for his production of Fokine's *L'Epreuve d'Amour*, and of the Catalan painter, Andreu, for his productions of Fokine's *Don Juan* and *Jota Aragonesa*. From 1938 until 1942 the artistic direction of the company passed into the control of the choreographer, Massine. This led to the production of ballets with settings by C. Bérard, Berman, Emile Bertin, Stewart Chaney, Alvin Colt, Salvador Dali, E. Dunkel, N. Gontcharova, Rea Irwin, Henri Matisse, Pierre Roy, and Oliver Smith.

The Soviet Ballet, which suggests an illimitable field for experiment, has contributed little to the advancement of stage decoration, with the exception of the very interesting experiments in constructivism attempted by Anatol Petritsky at Kharkov. The decoration of most of the ballets presented at Moscow and Leningrad is frankly realistic, and frequently of no particular distinction. Here I should like to make an exception in favour of Bobyshov, Dmitriev, Rabinovich, and P. Williams.

The ballet company attached to the Paris Opera showed signs of renewed activity since Serge Lifar became *maître de ballet*. Three productions at least were of considerable artistic interest—*Sur le Borysthène* (1932), with settings and costumes by Goncharova and Larionov (1932), *Icare* (1935), with settings and costumes by Larthe (1935), and *David Triomphant* (1937), with settings and costumes by Fernand Léger.

From the choreographic standpoint one of the most interesting of recent ballets was *The Green Table* produced by Kurt Jooss at Paris in 1932. But, apart from the excellent masks designed by Hein Heckroth, it is not specially important from the decorative aspect, since, like most of Jooss's productions, it is given against a black velvet surround, the several changes being indicated by skilful lighting.

Another company of interest is the Latvian Ballet at Riga. Considering this national ballet was only founded in 1922 and has been built up under the greatest difficulties, it can be said to have made astonishing progress. Among the Latvian designers who have worked for this company must be mentioned Ludolfs Liberts, P. Rozlapa, N. Strunke, S. Vidbergs, and E. Vitols. Some of these settings and costumes, particularly those of Liberts, are remarkable for their suggestion of mood and their imaginative qualities.

The Royal Danish Ballet at Copenhagen has produced several ballets which are of particular interest, for instance, *Bolero*, with setting and costumes by Svend Johannsen, *Le Lac des Cygnes*, with setting by Poul Kannenworff, and *La Veuve dans la Miroir*, with setting and costumes by Kjeld Abell.

At Budapest the settings for the productions of the Royal Hungarian Opera Ballet have been mainly designed by Gusztav Oláh and Zoltan Fülöp, two artists endowed with unusually fertile imaginations and a rare feeling for design and decoration.

In Czechoslovakia there have been some unusual productions such as the *surréaliste* ballet *Songes*, with choreography by Milea Mayerova.

Italy has produced little experiment in modern forms. The most important pre-War settings were those designed for the Scala Theatre, Milan, by the Italian painters Prince Mario Filomarino and Antonio Rovescalli, and the Russian, Nicholas Benois, and those designed by the first-named for the ballets given at the Royal Theatre, Rome, and the San Carlo Theatre, Naples, then directed by Dr. Paolo Fabbri. The *Chamber Ballet of San Remo*, directed by Cia Fornaroli, presented settings for the miniature stage.

In the United States of America there has been a revival of interest in Ballet, and many of the productions of the last few years, particularly those sponsored by Adolph Bolm, the Chicago Opera Co., Michel Fokine, the Metropolitan Opera Co., the Mordkin Ballet, the Philadelphia Ballet, and the San Francisco Ballet, have frequently been distinguished for their settings, for which, until recently, Russian artists in America, such as Remisov and Sudeikine, were mainly responsible.

But the determined effort to found a national ballet—a movement which had its inception in 1933 and the honour of which belongs to Lincoln Kirstein and Edward M. Warburg—has resulted in a new series of productions often remarkable for the artistry of their settings and costumes, which have been entrusted for the most part to modern French and Russian painters. Among the designers associated with the *American Ballet*, later known as the *Ballet Caravan*, are Bérard, Cadmus, Chaney, Colt, Derain, Free, French, Halicka, Held, Lurçat, Rain, Sharaff, Sudeikine, Tchelichev, and Franklin Watkins.

Perhaps the most promising company in America to-day is the American sponsored but internationally constituted organisation known as *The Ballet Theatre*, which has its headquarters at New York, and already possesses a repertory of some thirty ballets, with settings and costumes designed by such well known artists as B. Aronson, L. Ballard, E. Berman, J. Castillanos, M. Chagall, A. Colt, M. Dobuzhinsky, Lundberg, J. Mielziner, N. de Molas, Motley, Lee Simonson, and M. Vertes.

In England, among the first modern English painters to design scenery for ballet were Albert Rutherston and S. H. Sime, both of whom contributed settings and costumes for the Pavlova Company; George Sheringham, who devised the dresses for *The Swinburne Ballet* (1917); Paul Nash, who devised the setting and costumes for Barrie's play with ballet—*The Truth about the Russian Dancers* (1920); and C. Lovat Fraser, who planned several costumes for Mme. Karsavina's season at the Coliseum (1921).

The foundation of the Camargo Society in 1931 not only gave an impetus to the development of English choreographers and dancers, but afforded native-born artists an opportunity of designing for the Ballet. Although the Society expired in 1933, it can look back upon a period of undoubted service towards the promotion of English ballet, and can cite an interesting selection of painters associated with its productions, for instance, John Armstrong, Vanessa Bell, Edward Burra, William Chappell, Duncan Grant, Gwendolen Raverat, and George Sheringham.

The establishment of the Vic-Wells Ballet by Lilian Baylis and Ninette de Valois in 1931, and that of the Ballet Club by Marie Rambert in the same year, provided what it is to be hoped will prove to be permanent centres of Ballet in this country. Both directors have chosen their artistic collaborators with care, and many artistically interesting productions have been given by these two companies. The principal designers associated with the Vic-Wells Ballet, now styled the Sadlers's Wells Ballet, are John Armstrong, Cecil Beaton, Nadia Benois, Lord Berners, Hedley Briggs, Edward Burra, William Chappell, Phyllis Dolton, Sophie Fedorovich, Roger Furse, Leslie Hurry, E. McKnight Kauffer, Oliver Messel, Motley, John Piper, Hugh Stevenson, Rex Whistler, and Chiang Yee; while the artists associated with the Ballet Club include Nadia Benois, William Chappell, Sophie Fedorovich, Andrée Howard, Susan Salaman, and Hugh Stevenson.

The Markova-Dolin Company, which endured from 1935 to 1937, produced at least three scenically interesting works in Meninsky's setting and costumes for *David*, those of Motley for *Aucassin and Nicolette*, and those by Kirsta for *La Bien Aimée*.

The Ballet Guild, founded 1941, the decorative side of whose productions has to be contrived within the bounds of rigid economy, has for designers Beryl Dean, Joan Jefferson Farjeon, Sylvia Green, and Joseph Carl.

The International Ballet, founded 1942, which has Doris Zinkeisen as its principal designer, has also presented ballets with settings and costumes by William Chappell, Sophie Fedorovich, H. Heckroth, Korovine, and Rex Whistler.

What is the function of the stage setting in relation to Ballet? Primarily, it is a background for the dancer, but that setting has to suggest the period, the place, and, most important of all, the mood of the ballet. And so the scene is invested with meaning by the application of form, decorative design, and colour.

Ballet is a complex art not fully savoured unless allied to its sister arts of music and painting, and the success of the complete work depends a great deal on the value of their co-operation, for inartistic scenery or costumes can mar a ballet just as much as poor choreography or bad dancing.

In general, the ideal scene is a painted back-cloth used in conjunction with suitable wings or cut-cloths, for this permits the attainment of the highest degree of poetic illusion, an essential quality, for the world of ballet is the domain of the unreal, and this type of setting frees the greatest area of the stage, an important consideration where dancing is concerned.

The scene can also take part in the ballet, for instance, the lines of the design can be repeated in the movements of the dancers. In the same way the scene can be used to reduce the dancers in size or, alternatively, accord them added height. The setting can concentrate attention on the dancer by throwing her into relief, or, failing sufficient contrast between costume and setting, reduce her to semi-obscurity.

There is a growing tendency in some quarters to make the setting felt rather than seen, to use a back-cloth in which decorative design is reduced to a minimum, the cloth being painted in one flat tone, or a succession of broken tones, sometimes in shades of the same colour, sometimes in two or three contrasted tints. This is the type of setting used in *Le Tricorne*, *Choreartium*, *Symphonie Fantastique*, and in many of the settings by Fedorovich seen at Sadler's Wells and at the New Theatre.

Costume for ballet is governed by five considerations: line, decorative design, colour, material, and relation to the dancer's movements. Again, the designer must always bear in mind that the costume worn by a dancer will be seen mainly under conditions of movement, often very rapid.

For a work conceived in the style of the pure classical ballet, the ballet-skirt, pink tights, and satin shoes are *de rigeur*, and if it be desired to suggest a particular period or setting, it is possible to introduce appropriate variations in cut and design which, in the hands of a skilful artist, can be very attractive. Admittedly, the use of ballet-shoes with dresses of certain epochs can strike a discordant note, but, since certain forms of traditional technique depend on the ballet-shoe, a concession must sometimes be made to a convention born of necessity.

When the ballet has an element of national dancing, there are splendid opportunities to contrive costumes suggesting national dress. Examples of such types are found in *Petrouchka*, *Le Tricorne*, *La Jarre*, *La Nuit de St. Jean*, and so forth.

Costume can play a considerable part in a ballet; it can assist the dancer in the creation of a character, emphasise line, and confer strength or softness according to its cut and material. Even a comparatively insignificant article of dress such as the white gloves by Chiarina and her friends in the *pas de trois*, " *Chopin*," in Fokine's *Le Carnaval* can be become so important that the dance is ruined if the gloves be made of another colour.

Further the dancer's costume must be designed with a view not only to the theme and period of the ballet, but in relation to what the dancer is required to do, for a costume made of unsuitable material can make the dancer as leaden-footed as a diver beneath the sea; a faulty sleeve will restrict a movement that should be full, or perhaps suggest the defect of raised shoulders; while a badly-designed head-dress can prevent the execution of certain turning movements which depend on balance and control. These are merely a few examples by the way.

One more point. It is most important, particularly in the case of a soloist, that the costume should be planned with careful regard to her physical structure, for, since few human beings are perfectly proportioned, minor defects can often be smoothed away by skilful planning, just as they can easily become intensified for lack of it.

Of late years the vogue for athleticism has led to the theory that the best costume for the male dancer is none. One school prefers the dancer's dress to be reduced to the minimum compatible with decency, so that the costume consists of little more than abbreviated shorts combined with a vest or miniature cape flung over the shoulders; another school favours the fleshings borrowed from the acrobat. These types, used in moderation, have much to commend them, but, exploited to excess, they become tedious. Certainly the dancer attains an ideal quality of freedom in his movements, but not without a certain loss of effect for the designer's invention is restricted, and the pleasing variety of shapes resulting from a well-planned costume is completely lost.

When the costumes have been roughed out, they must then be thought of in relation to the setting, so that one contributes to the other, while, together, they form an harmonious entity. Bakst, when designing a setting, used to say that it corresponded to a picture where the figures had still to be painted in.

The problem of establishing a nice balance between costume and setting is complicated in proportion to the number of costumes seen on the stage at one time, and according to their proximity or distance apart. Again, it is important to visualise the possible effect on the spectator of a costume or set of costumes, when followed, at a short interval, by another and different costume or set of costumes.

. . . .

The possibilities of Ballet to-day are immense; it is a most adaptable medium. Even in the eighteenth century Noverre observed that "a *maître de ballet* ought to explore everything, to examine all, since everything that exists in the universe can serve him as a model." And this dictum is truer still to-day when Ballet has become a vastly more comprehensive and more expressive art.

The steady growth of public interest has resulted in an increasing number of works being produced, particularly in England and America, a happy state of affairs which, if the promise be maintained, should afford designers a new field of endeavour; and, in the case of those who, by observation and study, have sought to fit themselves for the task, an opportunity to make their own contribution to the advancement of Ballet which, as already stated, is a composite branch of the Theatre in which choreography, music, *and painting* each and all play their part.

CYRIL W. BEAUMONT

Beaujoyeux's "Ballet Comique de la Reine" as performed at the Salle du Petit Bourbon, Paris,
1581. From a lithograph after an illustration to book of same name published at Paris, 1582.

A very interesting example of the *décor simultané* or multiple setting as applied to ballet. The spectators are seated on either side of the hall, while in the foreground are Henri III and the Queen-Mother, with their attendant nobles, ladies, and guards. To the right is the Grove of Pan, to the left a gilded arch covered with gleaming clouds; while in the far distance is a Grotto adorned with trees and filled with flowers and beasts, and behind that, Circe's Palace. In the left background can be seen a triumphal car. The illustration shows the opening of the ballet when a captive nobleman, having escaped from Circe's garden, tells the audience of his adventures.

*Setting by Giulio Parigi for " The Garden of Calypso," in " Il Giudito di Paride."   Music drama performed
at Florence, 1608, in honour of marriage of Grand Duke, Cosimo II, to Archduchess Mary Magdalene of Austria*

Costumes for dancers in the " Grand Ballet" in " Le Château de Bicêtre," 1632.

The ballets of Louis XIII invariably concluded with the most splendid *entrée* of all, called the *Grand Ballet*, a group
of dancers dressed alike in rich brocaded costumes *à la romaine*, black or gold masks, and headdresses adorned with
plumes or tinselled aigrettes.   These dancers, often led by the King himself, danced a set of figures generally containing some complimentary allusion.

Biblio. Nationale, Paris

Costumes for the Hermaphrodites in " La Douarière de Billebahaut."   Ballet performed at the Louvre, Paris, 1629.

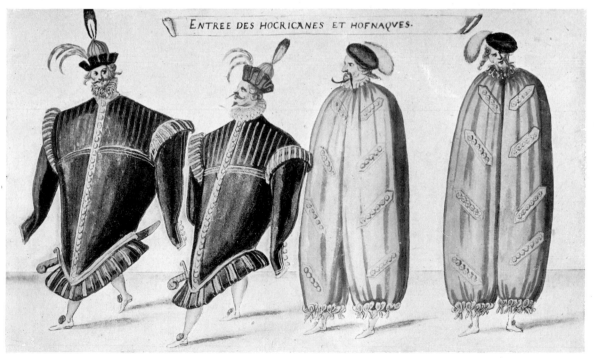

Biblio. Nationale, Paris

Costumes for the " Hocricanes " and " Hofnaques " in " La Douarière de Billebahaut " (Bilbao).

The costumes shown on this page are typical of the grotesque conceptions so frequently to be found in the ballets given at Court by Louis XIII. and his friends. The upper costumes are a curious mixture of European and Indian dress—feathers being generally used to suggest lightness or Indians, the warlike club and gentle distaff symbolising respectively the male and female elements. The lower designs are successful attempts to achieve an unusual, and droll effect by making a single article of attire do duty for a whole costume.

3

Setting for Oberon's Palace in " Oberon, the Faery Queen."   By Ben Jonson.   Performed 1611.

Setting for Luminalia, or the Festival of Light.   Scene 1, Night.   By Sir William Davenant.   Performed 1638.

The upper design shows the palace revealed after the opening of the first pair of shutters painted to resemble a mass of rocks.   Later the palace itself parts to discover the land of the fairies.   The lower design consists of four wings painted to represent trees, the " prospect " being a stretch of water which reflects the distant bank and the rising moon.

Copyright of the Duke of Devonshire

Costume for the King or a Masquer in
"Salmacida Spolia," by Sir William
Davenant. Performed 1640.

Copyright of the Duke of Devonshire

Costume for a Page, like a Fiery Spirit,
in "Lords Maske," by Thomas Campion.
Performed 1613.

Copyright of the Duke of Devonshire

Costume for Tethys in "Tethys Festival,"
by Samuel Daniel. Performed 1610.

Copyright of the Duke of Devonshire

Costume for the Spring in "Chloridia," by Ben Jonson.
Performed 1631.

The upper design is a variation of the costume *à la romaine*, but unusual in that the bases are padded. The chief interest of the costume for Tethys (Thetis) is the shell headdress, from which depends a floating veil, and the unusual ornamentation based on shell, sea-weed, and dolphin forms. The Fiery Spirit is reminiscent of Blake with its smoke mantle, and flame-like wings and bases.

5

Costume for Nobleman in " Ballet Royal de la Nuit," 1653.

Fantastic version of contemporary court dress.

Costume for Louis XIV as King Sun in " Ballet Royal de la Nuit."

An unusual example of the costume *à la romaine* in which Louis XIV's device of the sun and its rays supplies the decorative motif throughout.

Scene from " La Liberazione di Tirreno," ballet danced at Florence, 1616.   From the etching by Jacques Callot after Giulio Parigi.

This representation shows the symmetrical basis of choreography at this period.   Note the three planes—the dancers on the main floor, those on the stage, and those revealed in " cloud machines " lowered from the " flies."

Costumes for Aethiopians.

Costumes for Africans.

The costumes in the upper plate afford an invaluable lesson in the possibilities of applied decoration. The foundation garments are comparatively simple, but the unusual loop-like decoration in the one case, and the net-like over-design of woollen strands in the other instance, afford these costumes a most bizarre and unusual appearance. In the lower plate it is the fantastic cut of the garments themselves with their bright hues, that play so important a part in the piquant combination of the exotic and the barbaric, that forms the prime attraction of these costumes.

Autumn in " Les Fêtes de Bacchus."

A Soothsayer in " Les Fêtes de Bacchus."

Costume for Apollo in " Les Noces de Thétis et Pélée," 1654.

Costume for Persons in search of Rhythm which Wine has made them lose, in " Les Noces de Thétis et Pélée,' 1654.

Four costumes typical of those worn in ballets produced during the early years of the reign of Louis XIV. Until the performance of " Le Triomphe de l'Amour," 1681, all characters, both male and female, were sustained by men. It was far easier for men of slender build and wearing masks to portray women, than for women in the late nineteenth century to take masculine roles.

Biblio. de l'Arsenal, Paris

Costumes for the famous horse ballet known as " Le Carrousel de Louis XIV, 1662."

The lower plate depicts footmen in the quadrille of " Turks."   The upper plate shows footmen who escort led horses in the quadrille of " Indians."

Biblio. de l'Arsenal, Paris

Costume for the Duc de Guise as " King of the Americans " in the famous
horse-ballet known as " La Carrousel de Louis XIV," 1662.

The dress is an adaptation of the costume *à la romaine*, the " King " being conceived as a terrifying personage, his horse's mane and tail formed of writhing serpents, while in his hand he bears a mace and scourge fashioned of larger snakes.   The rider's saddlecloth is of tiger-skin bordered with gold, his costume and the horse's trappings are green and gold, the plumes which deck his helmet are green and white.

Costume for Mystery in " Le Triomphe de l' Amour."
Ballet by Benserade and Quinault with music by Lully.
Presented at Académie Royale de Musique, Paris, 1681.

Costume for Hermione in " Cadmus et Hermione." Lyric
tragedy by Quinault with music by Lully.   Presented
at Académie Royale de Musique, Paris, 1674.

Costume for a Bacchante.

Costume for the Indians in " Le Triomphe de l' Amour."

Berain's conceptions are remarkable for their air of distinction, their beautiful line, and their refined symbolism.
His costumes are obviously intended to be worn by persons of quality and are frequently theatricalised adaptations
of contemporary Court dress with borrowings from the costumes of ancient Rome.   Every detail is the object of
Berain's loving care and a fresh opportunity for the exercise of his artistic invention.

Costume for a Shoemaker.

Costume for an Architect. (Engravings by Jacques Le Pautre.)

Costume for a Silversmith.

Costume for Music. (Engravings by Jacques Le Pautre.)

Four examples of symbolist ballet costumes—Louis XIV period—in which the dress is formed from instruments and products associated with a particular trade or profession. This practice was recently revived by Giorgio di Chirico in his costumes for Massine's ballet, "Le Bal," (1929) in which architectural details were introduced.

Court Ballet danced before Louis XIV and the Princesse de Conti in 1683.   From the engraving by Le Pautre after Jean Berain.

Scene from " Alceste."   Lyrical Tragedy with entrées de ballet.   Presented in the court of the Palace of Versailles, 1676.   From the engraving by Le Pautre.

Costume for a Triton.

Costume for a River.

Costume for a Deity of the Underworld.

Costume for a Fury.

The Triton's costume is formed of algae and fish-like scales; his head-dress is a sea-plant adorned with branches of coral. The River shows a different arrangement of the same decorative motifs, the flow of the water being indicated by the trailing cloak. In the two lower costumes it is interesting to compare the varied use of Gorgon's heads.

Ballon.
From the engraving by H. Bonnart.

Mlle. Subligny.
From the engraving by H. Bonnart.

A Chinese.
From the engraving by H. Bonnart.

Mlle. Dufort as Folly.
From the engraving by Pierre le Pautre, after Berain.

In the previous pages the reader will have seen many costume designs for ballet dancers. Here are some contemporary studies of dancers wearing such costumes, which have clearly been designed by Berain or under his influence. The two upper designs are for dancers in the noble style. Ballon and Subligny were famous dancers of this period, the former being especially noted for his prodigious lightness.

Costume for the Hours of Night.

Costume for Folly.

Costume for a Naiad.

Costume for a Triton.

All the above costumes were designed for " Les Quatre Eléments," a ballet presented at the Palace of the Tuileries, Paris, 1721, and in which the King (Louis XV) took part. The most interesting of these costumes is that for Folly, which, with its tiers of flounces, certainly suggests frivolity. The " Hours " dress shows less invention. The two lower costumes are clearly influenced by Berain, but how simple and almost crude they are in comparison with that artist's creations. Note, however, the stiffened skirt or *tonnelet* worn by the Triton, which is to be typical of the costume for the male dancer in the noble style.

Design for a stage setting.

An example of the scientific principles of perspective as applied by an artist of genius to the creation of a lovely background for ballet.   Although the design is symmetrical, all sense of cold formality is dispelled by the warmth and colour produced by the introduction of skilfully contrasted masses of light and shade.   The dancers, in the serious or noble style, are wearing the traditional costume *à la romaine*.   No one has excelled the Bibiena family in the noble fantasy and supreme magnificence of their regal palaces and palace gardens.   Bakst himself consulted their designs when he sought inspiration for his settings for the Diaghilev revival of " La Belle au Bois Dormant " in 1921.

Costume for a Village Gallant as in " La Provençale "
and similar ballets.

Costume for a Chinese in " Les Indes Galantes," ballet
by Fuzelier with music by Rameau.   First performed
at Académie Royale de Musique, Paris, 1735.

Costume for a Village Belle as in " La Provençale "
and similar ballets.

Costume for a Chinese in " Les Indes Galantes " and
other ballets.

Examples of Martin's gay adaptations of peasant dress for a sophisticated pastoral ballet, and two charming conceptions of Chinese costume.   *Chinoiserie* of all kinds was greatly in vogue during the eighteenth century.   These costumes have served as inspiration to many later designers.

Costume for a Sylphide in the " Ballet des Eléments."

Costume for a Sylph in the " Ballet des Eléments."

Costume for a Fury in " Iphigénie en Tauride " and other operas.

Coll.: Doris Niles and Serge Leslie

Costume for a Demon in " Armide," " Psyche," and other operas.

Two sets of costumes for dancers in the noble style.   The upper pair are unusually simple, the principal decoration being cloud forms and small peacocks' feathers to symbolise lightness.   The *tonnelet* worn by the male dancer is of the later elliptical type.   The lower pair show a Fury and accompanying Demon.   The colours of these costumes suggest smoke and flame, the bodice and coat being black, the skirt and *tonnelet* red.   The ornamental design consists of Gorgons' heads and writhing serpents in green and gold.   The serpents, dagger, and torch held by the dancers are the attributes of Hate and therefore appropriate to Demons and Furies.

Costume for a Faun

Costume for Neptune.

Costume for an African.

Costume for Apollo.

In all the above designs it is of interest to note how the basic costume of plumed helmet and tunic with " tonnelet " is adapted by varying the decorative attributes and type of mantle to convey four totally different kinds of character. Part of Faun's costume is draped and spotted to suggest a wild animal's skin, the effect heightened by the claws placed on the " tonnelet." Neptune's costume is decorated with charming arrangements of sea plants, coral and shells of several sizes. Feathers are the accepted attribute of the natives of Africa, India and America. The costume for Apollo is a superb creation.

Trick Costume.   A dancer with two faces.

Male and female Pulcinella.

Trick costume to suggest two dancers.

Male and female Narcisino.

All the above designs are from the engravings by J. G. Puschner to " Neue & Curieuse Theatricalische Tantz-Schul," by Gregorio Lambranzi, published 1716.   This volume, a kind of ballet-master's hand-book, is intended to afford inspiration for dances of various types and includes some very unusual devices.   The two left-hand designs are trick costumes.   The upper figure has a mask at the back of the head, while the back of the coat is cut as in front, so that the dancer, even when actually dancing with his back to the audience, appears to be facing it.   In the lower costume, a male dancer wears a basket round his waist, to which is attached a woman's skirt ; the woman's head and shoulders is a dummy figure attached to the basket.   The two sets of costumes on the right are inspired by the masks of the *Commedia dell'Arte* ; the lower pair are the more unusual.   The huge hats are made of straw, the " eyes " formed from orange peel, while the nose was sometimes given a comical appearance by the addition of a piece of pumpkin.

Mask worn by a dancer at the opera, eighteenth century.
The mask is made of leather and represents a Faun.
The original mould of carved wood is also shown.

Mask worn by a dancer at the opera, eighteenth century.
The mask represents an Old Man.

Mask worn by a dancer at the opera, eighteenth century.
The mask presumably represents a Rustic.

Costume for a ballet dancer. From the engraving
by Mariette after Jean Berain.

Costume for a ballet dancer at the opera.
Engraving after Jean Berain.

In the late seventeenth and early eighteenth centuries the mask was regarded as an essential part of the dancer's costume. Not only did the mask vary in contour, but also in colour, for instance, those of Fauns were painted a blackish brown, those of Tritons green and silver, and those of Demons red and silver.

Costume for M. Gardel in "Hippomène et Atalante"
1749.

Costume for Mlle. Perceval in "Zoroastre." Presented at Académie Royale de Musique, Paris, 1749 (Revival of 1769).

Costume for Mlle. Asselin in "Hippomène et Atalante."

Costume for Diana in "Les Surprises de l'Amour." Presented: Académie Royale de Musique, Paris, 1757.

The above costumes, reproduced from the copies made by A. Guillaumot the Younger, are typical of those worn by dancers in the noble style.   That for Gardel shows the familiar dress *à la romaine* as worn at this period, the plumed helmet is adapted from Le Brun's paintings of Alexander.   The costume for Mlle. Perceval is trimmed with plumes, symbolical of lightness.   Mlle. Catinon's dress is indicative of her role as Diana.   Note the symbolic crescent ornament in her hair and the bodice coloured and spotted to suggest a wild animal's skin (cf. p. 21, costume for Faun).

Costume for Mlle. Lionnois in " Les Festes de l'Hymen et de l'Amour."   Académie Royale de Musique, Paris, 1769.

Costume for M. Lionnois in " Les Festes de l'Hymen et de l'Amour."

Costume for M. Malter in " La Provençale."
Presented at Académie Royale de Musique, Paris, 1769.

Costume for Mlle. Pitrot in " La Provençale."

Two sets of costumes for pastoral ballets, reproduced from copies made by A. Guillaumot the Younger.   The upper pair are in the noble style, the suggestion of rusticity being symbolised, in the case of the *danseuse*, by her sickle and the garlands formed from poppies and ears of wheat, while the *danseur* carries a sheaf of corn.   The lower set of costumes are theatricalised versions of peasant dress and clearly intended for a *pas villageois*.

Setting based on fountains beneath a portico.

Photos : Arch. Photog. d'Art et d'Histoire, Paris

Setting for a ballet on a Chinese theme.

Note the gaiety and comparative simplicity of Boquet's conceptions in contrast with the formal palatial Augustan edifices depicted in so many eighteenth-century settings for ballet.

Study of Salvatore Viganò (1769-1821).

Viganò's costume consists of white stockings and white close-fitting breeches, and a light short-sleeved coat with flared skirts. The coat is usually pale blue or deep pink, lined with white and bound with a white sash tied in a bow at the back in such a way as to leave long flowing ends. The flowing collar is also unusual. So far as can be ascertained, this particular style of coat is peculiar to Viganò.

The prime interest of these drawings from the viewpoint of costume is the simple dress of semi-transparent material, gathered beneath the breasts, worn by the *danseuse*, which was inspired by the Graeco-Roman fashions ushered in by the French Revolution. No costume could afford a greater contrast to those worn by the dancers of Louis XV and XVI. Note that the sandals have no heels.

Study of Salvatore Viganò and his wife—Marie Medina.

Setting for "Psammi re d Egitto." Ballet with choreography by Salvatore Viganò. Presented at Teatro alla Scala, Milan, 1817.

A scene in ancient Egypt showing the effect produced by the shifting of the viewpoint from the centre.

Setting for "Gli Strelizzi," Act V. Ballet with choreography by Salvatore Viganò. Presented at Teatro alla Scala, Milan, 1809.

Note the use of atmospheric lighting to establish a dramatic mood by affording contrasting masses of light and shade.

Costume for Pleasure (M. Vestris).

Costume for Elemental Spirit in " Zénis et Almasie." Ballet Héroique by Chamfort, with music by De Laborde and De Bury. Presented at Fontainebleau, 1765.

Costume for Rustic in " Don Quichotte chez la Duchesse."

Costume for Shepherdess (Mlle. Allard) in " Don Quichotte chez la Duchesse." Ballet Comique by Favart with music by Boismortier. Presented at Académie Royale de Musique, Paris, 1743.

The upper two designs are typical of costumes in the noble style. The *tonnelet* worn by the male dancer is an exaggerated example of the later elliptical form. The two lower designs are for pastoral ballets, these dresses being for *pas de caractère*.

From the Lithographs by G. Engelmann

Costumes for première danseuse and premier danseur in " Pas Gracieux " in "Aladin ou la Lampe Merveilleuse."
Opéra féerie with music by Nicolo Isonard. Presented at Académie Royale de Musique (Opéra), Paris, 1822.

From the Lithographs by G. Engelmann

Costume for a Nobleman and Bette in " Clari," ballet-pantomime with music by Kreutzer,
choreography by Milon. Presented at Académie Royale de Musique (Opéra), Paris, 1820.

The costume for female ballet dancers of the early nineteenth century is a theatricalised version of the women's dress at this period—the short-sleeved sheath-like frock of one piece reaching to the ankle and gathered under the breasts, which made its appearance during the First Empire. The low neck is very *décolletée*. The shoes have no heels. In the upper designs the costumes are given an Oriental character by the addition of jewelled embroidery, a form of decoration to which Garnerey was partial and which he used when occasion offered, as in " Aladin," with taste and distinction. The male dancer's costume is inspired by Renaissance fashions, and generally consists of a shirt, trunks, long-sleeved doublet, tights, and a feathered brimmed hat.

Coll.: W. Beaumont Morris

An " Indian " *pas de trois* as presented by the ballet company directed by Filippo Taglioni during their visit to Stuttgart, 1826. The women's costumes are merely shortened versions of Empire dresses, worn over Turkish trousers, probably inspired by those worn in Racine's play, *Bajazet*. The ostrich feather head-dresses are presumably a concession to the 17th century tradition which required " Indians " in ballet to be adorned with feathers. (cf. pages 10 and 12.)

Sword and Lance, a martial *pas de quatre*, as presented by the same company. Note the adaptation of Graeco-Roman costumes to the service of ballet. The Amazons are interesting as a precursor of the female warrior, a new conception to be exploited later with great effect in F. Taglioni's ballet, *La Révolte au Sérail*, 1833 (cf. page 37). Both illustrations are reproduced from the rare booklet, *Erinnerungen an das Ballet des Königlichen Hoftheaters zu Stuttgart*, 1826.

Biblio. de l'Opéra, Paris

Costume for a Peasant in the ballet in " Guillaume Tell," opera by Rossini. Presented at Académie Royale de Musique, Paris, 1829.

Costume for a Peasant Girl in the ballet in " Guillaume Tell."

Biblio. de l'Opéra, Paris

Costume for Zoloe (Mlle. Taglioni) in the ballet in " Le Dieu et la Bayadère," opera by Auber. Presented : Académie Royale de Musique, Paris, 1830.

Costume for Ninka in " Le Dieu et la Bayadère."

The ballet in " Guillaume Tell," with its choreography by F. Taglioni, has a special interest in that it is believed to mark the first occasion when the national dance forms of other countries—in this case Switzerland—were adapted to the service of ballet. This innovation is credited to Marie Taglioni. The costumes, obviously based on authentic sources, are charming. The Indian dresses, too, are distinguished by their refinement and a regard for correct detail which was rare at this period.

Mlle. Noblet in " La Paysanne Supposée." (Published 1822.) Ballet with choreography by Deshayes. Presented : King's Theatre, London, 1821.

From the lithograph after Levasseur

Mme. Brugnoli and Sig. Samingo in " L'Anneau Magique." Presented : King's Theatre, London, 1832.

From the lithograph by and after F. Waldeck (pub. 1821)

Mlle. Fanny Bias in "Flore et Zéphire." Presented : King's Theatre, London.

From the lithograph after A. E. Chalon (pub. 1831)

Marie Taglioni as Flore in " Flore et Zéphire." Ballet by Didelot. Presented : King's Theatre, London, 1830.

The lower plates show theatricalised versions of contemporary costume as worn by *ballerine* in the mythological ballets then fashionable. The upper right plate shows *demi-caractère* costumes, that of the female dancer being adapted from contemporary dress, that of the male dancer showing the influence of Renaissance styles. The upper left plate shows the theatricalised peasant dress worn by dancers in ballets on village themes.

From the series of costume plates pub. Hautecoeur, Martinet, Paris

M. and Mme. Paul Taglioni in the Pas Styrien in "Gustave III ou le Bal Masqué," Act V. Opera by Auber. Pres.: Académie Royale de Musique, Paris, 1833. Costume inspired by Styrian peasant dress.

Marie Taglioni as Nathalie in "Nathalie ou la Laitiére Suisse." Ballet with choreography by F. Taglioni. Pres.: Académie Royale de Musique, Paris, 1832. Costume inspired by Swiss peasant dress.

From the series of plates pub. Hautecoeur, Martinet, Paris

Mabille and Mlle. Dumilâtre in " La Péri." Ballet by T. Gautier with choreography by J. Coralli. Pres.: Académie Royale de Musique, Paris, 1843. Although the ballet is set in Cairo, the costumes are inspired by Balkan dress.

Fanny Elssler as Mathilde in " L'Ile des Pirates," Act II. Ballet-pantomime by A. Nourrit with music by Carlini, Gide, etc., and choreography by Henry. Presented at Académie Royale de Musique, Paris, 1835.

From the lithograph by Deveria

Fanny Elssler in " Le Diable Boiteux."

From the lithograph by Alophe

Adeline Plunkett in " La Manola."

*Mlles. Danse and Ropiquet in the " Jaleo de Xeres,"
from " Le Diable Boiteux."*

From the lithograph by F. H. Lynch

Marie Guy Stéphan in " Las Boleras de Cadiz."

The triumph of Fanny Elssler's Cachuca in " La Diable Boiteux " (1836) and of the Spanish dances introduced into the last act of that ballet, together with the attractions of Spanish costumes, created a vogue for such dances. Above are typical examples of adaptations of Spanish costume. The skirt may be short or long and decorated with flounces of black lace, vertical lines of silver, or a vandyked over-skirt. The bodice is generally of satin or velvet, frequently of a different colour from that of the skirt, and may be plain or decorated with tasselled epaulets and gold or silver embroidery.

*First costume for
Duke Albrecht.*

Biblio. de l'Opéra, Paris

*Costume for Giselle
as Vinedresser.*

*Another design for
Giselle's costume, in-
teresting as showing the
clarity of Lormier's
technical instructions.*

Costume for Nobleman in Hunting Dress.

Second costume for Duke Albrecht.

Four costumes for " Giselle."   Ballet by T. Gautier, V. de St. Georges and J. Coralli ; with music by A. Adam and choreography by J. Coralli and Jules Perrot.   Presented at Académie Royale de Musique, Paris, 1841.   This ballet, still in the repertory of leading companies, is the only ballet which can trace an unbroken tradition of performance since its first production, now covering a period of over a hundred years.

Biblio. de l'Opéra, Paris

Costume for the dancers of the Csárdás in "Coppélia" Ballet with choreography by A. Saint-Léon. Presented at Théâtre Impérial de l'Opéra, Paris, 1870.

Costume for women dancers of the Csárdás in " Coppélia."

Costume for Dawn in " Coppélia."

Costume for Farfalla in " Le Papillon," Act I, Scene 1. Ballet with choreography by Marie Taglioni. Pres. : Théâtre Impérial de l'Opéra, Paris, 1861.

In the realistic type of the Romantic Ballet, the action was frequently set in some country which would permit of the introduction of attractive and unusual national dances, this practice continued until late in the nineteenth century. Such ballets included both character and classical " numbers," the dancers wearing accordingly costume based on national dress or the ballet skirt. The designs on this page show a classical ballet costume and two costumes based on Hungarian dress for " Coppélia," and the Caucasian costume worn by Farfalla as maid to the Fairy Hamza, in the first act of " Le Papillon."

Coll.: Harold Rubin

Costume for a Wilis in " Giselle."   *Mlle. Urban.*

Coll.: Harold Rubin

Mlle. Lamy   *Dancer unidentified.*

Examples of classical ballet costume as worn at the Paris Opera in the eighteen-sixties—some thirty years after its appearance in " La Sylphide " (see page 36).   The dress has become shorter and dome-shaped.   The upper right plate is interesting for its decoration of wild flowers and wheat ears.   The lower right plate shows the decorative use of ribbon, note also the charming arrangement of flowers in the dancer's hair.   The lower left plate shows a typical adaptation to suggest peasant dress.

Costume as worn in " Les Génies Elémentaires," 1765.

Costume for Mlle. Clotilde in " La Vallée de Tempé ou le retour de Zéphire." 1802.

Musée de l'Opéra, Paris

Costume worn by a dancer at the Opera, Paris, 1881.

These three costumes illustrate three important stages in the evolution of ballet costume during a period of just over a century. First, the dancer of the eighteenth century with her satin bodice and paniered skirt, her high feathered coiffure and heeled shoes. Second, the dancer of the beginning of the nineteenth century wearing the semi-transparent filmy robe, flowing hair, and heelless shoes ushered in by the French Revolution in imitation of the fashions of the Graeco-Roman republics. Third, the dancer wearing the classic Sylphide costume as it appeared some fifty years years after its introduction (see page 36).

Regatta at Venice.

The "Grand Prix" at Longchamps.

Ice Racing Carnival at Montreal.

Big Game Hunting.

The Triumph of Sport.

Five scenes from "Sport." Ballet by L. Manzotti, with music by R. Marenco and choreography by Luigi Manzotti. Presented at Teatro alla Scala, Milan, 1897.

Typical examples of the type of the realistic settings and costumes used in Manzotti's spectacular propagandist ballets. Note also the "danseuses de travestie" in the two top plates—the gondoliers in the first plate and the ladies' escorts in the second are women dressed as men.

Costume based on a Potato.

Costume based on a Cabbage.

Costume based on a Horsechestnut.

Costume based on a Radish.

Four examples of Croce's resource in adapting fruit and vegetable forms as drawn for dancers; obviously the dancing would be of the simplest kind.

Costume for the Bread-crumb Fairy and her Page. (Kulichevskaya and Kshesinsky.)

Costume for the White Cat. This and the facing costumes were designed by I. A. Vsevolozhsky.

Costume for the Lilac Fairy (Marie Petipa) and Pages.

A. M. Shishkov.   Setting for " La Belle au Bois Dormant," Prologue—The Christening.   Ballet with music by P. I. Tchaikovsky and choreography by Marius Petipa.   Presented at Maryinsky Theatre, St. Petersburg, 1890.

In this original production the Prologue and Act I were placed in the Valois period.   The later acts were set in the reign of Louis XIV.   The photograph is taken at the moment when the sinister fairy, Carabosse, makes her entrance in a curious vehicle shaped like a black cat.   In the background will be observed the rats who draw the carriage.   The scene is a built-up set, a realistic presentation of the interior of a Renaissance palace.   Note the " historical " costumes of the mimes and supers, and the convention which permits of the introduction of dancers wearing ballet-skirts.

Setting for " Le Lac des Cygnes." Act II. A lake-side with a ruined chapel.

Photos. by courtesy of Society for Cultural Relations with U.S.S.R.

Setting for " Le Lac des Cygnes," Act III—a splendid ballroom. Ballet by V. P. Begitchev and Geltser, with music by P. I. Tchaikovsky and choreography by Marius Petipa and L. I. Ivanov. Presented (first time in its entirety) at Maryinsky Theatre, St. Petersburg, 1895.

Realistic built-up sets typical of the productions of the Imperial Russian Ballet—last quarter of the nineteenth century.

Adaptation to suggest Italian national costume.

Adaptation to suggest Polish national costume.

*Anna Pavlova as the Spanish Doll in " The Fairy
Doll."   Adaptation to suggest Spanish national
costume.*

Spanish costume for male dancer.

48

Anna Pavlova and Michel Fokine as Javotte and Jean in " Javotte." Ballet with music by C. Saint-Saëns. Revival, pres. : Maryinsky Theatre, St. Petersburg.

Matilda Kshesinskaya as Esmeralda in " Esmeralda." Ballet with choreography by Jules Perrot. Revival, as presented at Maryinsky Theatre, St. Petersburg.

Anna Pavlova and Michel Fokine in " Arlequinade." Ballet with choreography by Marius Petipa. Presented at Maryinsky Theatre, St. Petersburg, 1900.

Anna Pavlova as Flore in " Le Réveil de Flore." Ballet with music by R. Drigo and choreography by Marius Petipa.

The two upper plates show the traditional ballet skirt adapted to suggest the costume of a French peasant girl, and a street dancer of the Middle Ages. The two lower plates represent an ingenious adaptation of eighteenth-century military costume, and a naïve attempt to suggest ancient Greece with a garland of flowers and an over-skirt decorated with a Greek key pattern. Note that in most cases the coiffure of the *danseuses* follows the pompadour style fashionable at the beginning of the twentieth century.

Marie M. Petipa and Sergey Legat in " La Fille du Pharaon." Choreography by

Marius Petipa. Revival, as presented at Maryinsky Theatre, St. Petersburg, 1890.

Photos. by Courtesy of Society for Cultural Relations with U.S.S.R.

Thamar Karsavina in the " Torch Dance " in " Une Nuit d'Egypte." Ballet with choreography by Michel Fokine. Presented at Maryinsky Theatre, St. Petersburg, 1908.

Vera Fokina as Ta Hor in " Cléopâtre." Revised version of "Une Nuit d'Egypte." The costume is by Leon Bakst. Pres. : Diaghilev Ballet Co., Théâtre du Chatelet, Paris, 1909.

The upper plate shows the traditional ballet skirt adapted by means of decoration based on Egyptian motifs to suggest an Egyptian woman in accordance with the conventions still existing early in the twentieth century. The left lower plate shows an endeavour to suggest something of a genuine costume of ancient Egypt. Note the elongated eyes and the wig made of tow, also the feet with shoes but in tights, for at this time bare feet would have been considered indecent. The lower right plate shows the arrival of a simple striped robe and actually bared legs and feet.

Marie M. Petipa and P. A. Gerdt in the Bacchanale from " Les Saisons."   Ballet with music by Glazunov and choreography by Marius Petipa.   Pres. at Maryinsky Theatre, St. Petersburg, 1900.

The upper plate shows the traditional ballet skirt adapted to suggest a Greek bacchante, the skirt being fringed with vine leaves and garlanded with clusters of grapes ; similar clusters fall over the shoulders and adorn the hair. Below is the result of the reforms initiated by Fokine. It is exactly the same " number," but now the danseuse wears a simple tunic of semi-transparent material (the costume was designed by Bakst), the hair is banded with a red ribbon, the ears coquettishly decorated with a cluster of grapes.

Anna Pavlova and Laurent Novikov in the " divertissement " " L'Autumne Bacchanale " from " Les Saisons." Revival circa 1911.

Costumes for " Old China."   Ballet by C. Wilhelm, with music by Leopold Wenzel and choreography by Katti Lanner.   Presented at Empire Theatre, London, 1901.

Examples of familiar types of china and porcelain adapted as costumes for dancers.

Costume for a Goldfish.

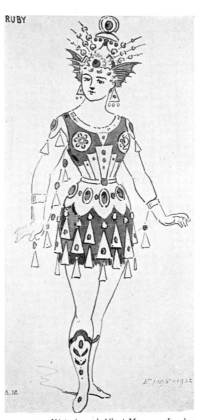

Victoria and Albert Museum, London

Costume to represent Rubies.

Costume for a Swallow.

Victoria and Albert Museum, London

Costume for a Lemon.

Costumes of the obvious or semi-realistic type, designed primarily to reveal the figure, and founded on a close-fitting garment covering the upper part of the body, trunks, and tights.

From " Winkles and Champagne," by M. Willson Disher

Scene from " L'Amour."   Ballet with music by François Thomé and choreography by Alfredo Curti.   Presented at Alhambra Theatre, London, 1906.

By courtesy of the Exp. des Ballets Russes de Diaghilev au Pav. de Marsan, Paris

Setting for " Cléopâtre."   Ballet with music by Arensky, etc., and choreography by Michel Fokine.   Revival as presented by Diaghilev Ballet Co., Théâtre du Chatelet, Paris, 1909.

Above is a typical example of the realistic school of scenic design contrasted with an example of the decorative school. Both seek to evoke the Orient of antiquity, " L'Amour " being set in Assyria and " Cléopâtre " in Egypt.   The first is an elaborate built-up set overcrowded with detail ; it is purely representational and establishes no mood.   The second, which is dominated by the giant figures hewn out of tawny rock, at once strikes a mood of grandeur and solemnity, proper to the drama to be enacted.

Courtesy of the Exp. des Ballets Russes de Diaghilev au Pav. de Marsan, Paris

Bakst. Spirit of the Rose (V. Nijinsky) in " Le Spectre de la Rose." Ballet with choreography by Michel Fokine. Pres. : Diaghilev Ballet Co., Théâtre de Monte Carlo, 1911.

Bakst. Costume for the Young Girl in " Le Spectre de la Rose " (T. Karsavina).

Courtesy of the Exp. des Ballets Russes de Diaghilev au Pav. de Marsan, Paris

Benois. Setting for "Les Sylphides." Choreography by Michel Fokine. Pres.: Diaghilev Ballet Co., Paris, 1909.

Bakst's costume for the Spirit of the Rose consisted of elastic silk fleshings—leaving the arms and breast bare—of a deep rose colour ; thighs flecked with a few greenish leaf-like shapes ; tunic almost covered with silk rose petals of varying hues ; on the head a cap of rose petals, with bracelets of petals banding the biceps. The original design for " Les Sylphides " is far superior to later settings by other designers.

Setting for " Le Pavillon d'Armide." Scene I.

Setting for " Le Pavillon d'Armide," Scene II. Ballet by A. Benois, with music by Nicholas Tcherepnine and choreography by Michel Fokine. Presented at the Maryinsky Theatre, St. Petersburg, 1907.

Note how the setting of the first scene, a charming composition of those baroque elements—classic urns, amorini, *oeils-de-boeuf*, draped curtains, and garlands of fruit and flowers—dear to the eighteenth-century architect—affords a contrast to the second scene with its formal hedges typical of the gardens designed by Le Nôtre and his followers.

Victoria and Albert Museum, London

Armide's Slave.

Costume for Armide and her Pages.

Costume for the Marquis.

Courtesy the Exp. des Ballets Russes de Diaghilev
au Pav. de Marsan, Paris

Costume for the Vicomte de Beaugency as René.

Costume for Florestan in "Le Carnaval."   *Costume for Pantalon in "Le Carnaval.*

*Ballet to music by Robert Schumann with choreography by Michel Fokine.   Presented at Pavlova Hall,
St. Petersburg, 1910.*

Costume for a Footman in "Papillons."   *Costume for a Young Girl in "Papillons."*

*Ballet to music by Robert Schumann with choreography by Michel Fokine.   Presented at Maryinsky Theatre,
St. Petersburg, 1912.*

Examples of Bakst costumes inspired by the elegant "Biedermeier" style typical of the eighteen-forties.

MITISLAV DOBUZHINSKY

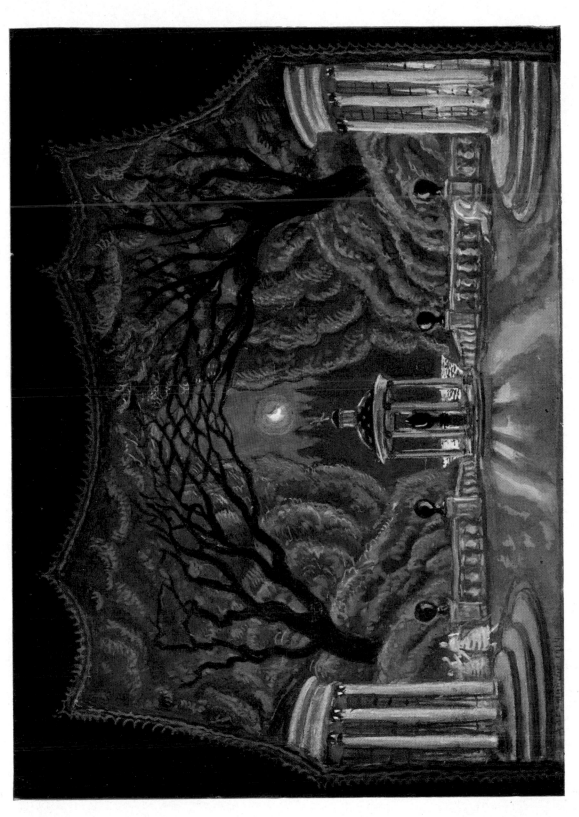

*Setting for " Papillons."   Ballet to music by Robert Schumann, with choreography by Michel Fokine.   Revival as presented by Diaghilev Ballet Co.,
Théâtre du Chatelet, Paris, 1912.*

A charming evocation of the romanticism of the eighteen-thirties, in which a love-lorn Pierrot, wandering in a park, mistakes for
butterflies some young ladies wearing yellow crinolines.   Note the effective simplicity of the composition, in which everything is
subordinated to the suggestion of mood, a final touch of mystery being contributed by the black cut-cloth curtain.

Courtesy of the Exp. des Ballets Russes de Diaghilev au Pav. de Marsan, Paris

Golovine. Backcloth for "L'Oiseau de Feu." Ballet with music by Igor Stravinsky and choreography by Michel Fokine. Pres.: Diaghilev Ballet Co., Théâtre Nationale de l'Opéra, Paris, 1910.

L. Bakst. Costume for the Firebird.   *Korovine. Costume for an Attendant on Kostchei.*

Golovine's setting for " L'Oiseau de Feu " has never been surpassed for its poetical suggestion of an enchanted wood, a land of eerie shadows except where gleams a magic tree laden with silver apples. Later comes the sudden blazing into light of the forest to reveal the enchanter's castle. Something of this magic can be gleaned from the plate above, but its lovely glowing colour must be imagined. The costumes are by Korovine with the exception of that for the Firebird, which was designed by Bakst. The Firebird costume is a fine conception—a women's head and shoulders emerging from a bird-like body of swansdown.

Benois.   Nursemaid and Coachman in " Petrouchka."   *Roehrich.   Costume for a Polovtsian Warrior.*

Victoria and Albert Museum, London

*Roehrich.   Setting for the Polovtsian Dances from " Prince Igor."   Ballet to music by Alexander Borodin, with
choreography by Michel Fokine.   Presented by the Diaghilev Ballet Co., Théâtre du Chatelet, Paris, 1909.*

There is no other stage designer who can equal Roehrich in the evocation of primitive Russia with its bleak landscapes
and suggestion of mingled savagery and mysticism.

Setting for " Petrouchka," Scene I.

Setting for " Petrouchka," Scene III.

In the upper scene Benois has evoked a famous quarter in the St. Petersburg of 1830—the Admiralty Square during Butter Week, a period of Carnival when entertainers and street-vendors of all kinds set up their stalls and booths in the Square. The lower scene shows the room of the Moor, whose character, already suggested by his costume, is emphasised by his florid surroundings. Note the setting consists of a permanent false proscenium frame, fitted with a drop curtain which is lowered during changes of scene. Ballet by Alexandre Benois and Igor Stravinsky, with music by I. Stravinsky and choreography by Michel Fokine. Presented by the Diaghilev Ballet, Théâtre du Chatelet, Paris, 1911.

Costume for the Moor.

Costume for a Street Dancer.

Costume for Petrouchka.

Costume for the Ballerina.

Four costumes for " Petrouchka." Three of the designs are for the principal characters—the three puppets which the Magician will invest with a brief existence. How charming their costumes are and how well contrasted. Note the florid clumsy Moor who wears blue, green, and silver; plaintive Petrouchka in red and yellow; and the dainty Ballerina in maroon and pink.

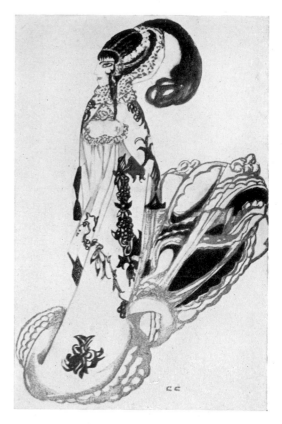

Negro Executioners in " La Tragédie de Salomé."
Choreography by Boris Romanov. Pres.: Diaghilev
Ballet Co., Théâtre des Champs Elysées, 1913.

Costume for Salomé in " La Tragédie de Salomé."
Both illustrations are designs by S. Sudeikine.

Courtesy of the Exp. des Ballets Russes de Diaghilev au Pav. de Marsan, Paris

L. Bakst. Setting for " Jeux." Ballet to music by Claude Debussy, with choreography by Vaslav Nijinsky.
Presented by Diaghilev Ballet Co., Théâtre des Champs Elysées, Paris, 1913.

Sudeikine's costumes for " La Tragédie de Salomé " are conceived in the decadent style of Beardsley's illustrations to Wilde's " Salomé." Bakst's setting presents a moonlit park in which a group of young people are to enjoy a game of tennis.

Costume for a Nymph.   *Costume for the Faun (V. Nijinsky).*

Courtesy of the Exp. des Ballets Russes de Diaghilev au Pav. de Marsan, Paris

Setting for " L'Après-Midi d'un Faune."   Ballet by Leon Bakst to music by Claude Debussy, with choreography by Vaslav Nijinsky.   Presented by Diaghilev Ballet Co., Théâtre du Chatelet, Paris, 1912.

Bakst had a particular affection for the Greece of antiquity, and in his setting and costumes for this ballet he has re-captured something of that loveliness which so many poets honoured in song.   The cool white pleated robes of the nymphs make a living frieze as the dancers glide past the sun-drenched foliage of the backcloth.   Of all Bakst's designs there is none more beautiful than that of the Faun slaking his thirst with a handful of grapes.   The ballet-goer will be able to form some idea of how much this ballet loses when the scenery is limited to a crude suggestion of rock.

Costume for a Hamadryad in " Midas."

Costume for Apollo in " Midas."

Setting for " Midas."   Ballet by Léon Bakst, with music by Maximilian Steinberg and choreography by Michel Fokine.   Presented by Diaghilev Ballet Co., Théâtre National de l'Opéra, Paris, 1914.

The artist has sought to convey an appropriate setting for the classic theme by presenting a landscape in the manner of the Italian painters of the early Renaissance.

LEON BAKST

Musée des Arts Décoratifs, Paris

Setting for "Schéhérazade." Ballet by Léon Bakst, with music by N. Rimsky-Korsakow, and choreography by Michel Fokine.
Presented by the Diaghilev Ballet Co., Théâtre National de l'Opéra, Paris, 1910.

A masterpiece of stage design which conjures up all the Oriental splendour, sensuality, and cruelty of the first tale of "The Thousand and One Nights." Note the importance of the great swirling folds of green curtain in the evocation of a voluptuous mood, just as the tragic note is struck by the violent contrast of the blood-red carpet. Relatively considered, there is very little detail, the whole effect of the setting being achieved by its wonderful massing of colour.

L. Bakst.   Costume for a Negro.   L. Bakst.   Costume for Potiphar's Wife.

Sert.   Scene from " La Légende de Joseph."   Ballet by Hugo von Hoffmannsthal and Count Harry Kessler, with music by Richard Strauss and choreography by Michel Fokine.   Presented by Diaghilev Ballet Co., at Théâtre National de l'Opéra, Paris, 1914.

The decoration of this ballet is unusual.   The majority of the costumes, such as those above, were adapted from the paintings of Paolo Veronese, while the setting suggested both antiquity and magnificence, the walls being of gold and the convoluted columns of green shot with gold like the wing-cases of certain beetles.

Setting for " Le Sacre du Printemps," Scene I.   Ballet with music by Igor Stravinsky and choreography by Vaslav Nijinsky.   Presented by Diaghilev Ballet Co.   Théâtre National de l'Opéra, Paris, 1914.

Setting for " Le Sacre du Printemps," Scene II.

The upper design is a good example of Roehrich's artistry in composing and painting a landscape which is surcharged with primitiveness and mysticism.   The great clouds, filled with moisture, are very typical.

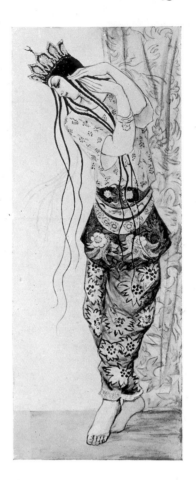

Natalia Goncharova. Costumes for "Le Coq d'Or" —Prince Guidon (left), and The Queen of Shemakhân (right).

Natalia Goncharova. Setting for "Le Coq d'Or," Act II, Scene I. Presented by the Diaghilev Ballet Co., Théâtre National de l'Opéra, Paris, 1914.

Setting for " Le Coq d'Or," Act I. Opera-Ballet by V. Bielsky, revised by Alexandre Benois, with music by N. Rimsky-Korsakov and choreography by Michel Fokine. Presented by the Diaghilev Ballet Co. at Théâtre National de l'Opéra, Paris, 1914.

This setting inaugurated a new phase of stage decoration inspired by the peasant arts of Russia and Persia. This vivid, violently contrasted colouring and the fantasy of the designs are decidedly original.

Costume for the Midnight Sun.   *Costume for a Young Girl.*

*Setting for " Soleil de Nuit " (The Midnight Sun).   Ballet to music by Rimsky-Korsakov, with choreography
by Leonide Massine.   Presented by Diaghilev Ballet Co., 1915.*

Larionov's first work for the Diaghilev Ballet.   The setting is a simple but most effective composition of a garland of
orange suns set against a rich blue sky.   The costumes are theatricalised interpretations of Russian peasant costumes.

Costume for Baba Yaga.

*Sketch showing plan of make-up
for Kikimora.*

Costume for Bova Korolevich.

*Setting for " Contes Russes " (Children's Tales), Scene I.   Ballet to music by Liadov, choreography by Leonide
Massine.   Presented by Diaghilev Ballet Co.   This ballet originally consisted of one scene.   Later, other episodes
were added, the complete work in four scenes and two interludes being given at the Coliseum Theatre, London, 1918.*

Larionov's settings and costumes, though quite distinctive, have the same vivid colour and the same strength and
fantasy of design as the conceptions of Goncharova, and derive from a close study of Russian folklore art adapted
to the service of the theatre.

*Hein Heckroth. Costumes for " Ballade." Ballet with music by John Colman; choreography by Kurt Jooss.
Presented by Ballets Jooss, Gaiety Theatre, London, 1935.*

(By courtesy of Theatre Arts Monthly)

*Robert Edmond Jones. Setting for " Tyl Eulenspiegel." Ballet with music by Richard Strauss; choreography
by Vaslav Nijinsky. Presented by the Diaghilev Ballet Co., New York, 1916.*

Costume for Constanza.　　　　　　　　*Costume for Count Rinaldo.*

Second setting for " Les Femmes de Bonne Humeur " (The Good Humoured Ladies).　Ballet to music by Scarlatti, with choreography by Leonide Massine.　Pres.: Diaghilev Ballet Co., Teatro Costanza, Rome, 1917

An evocation of eighteenth-century Venice which owes something to the paintings of Francesco Guardi.　How **well** Bakst suggests through the rich reds and browns of the houses, relieved by the gleaming campanile, the leisurely **life** of the town, which is to form the background for the coffee-house banter and carnival intrigue on which the **action** of the ballet is based.

Costume for the Dandy and a Peasant Girl in " Le Tricorne." Ballet with choreo-
graphy by L. Massine. Pres.: Diaghilev Ballet Co., Alhambra, London, 1919.

Setting for " Le Tricorne."

Almost all the costumes in this ballet are based on the decorative use of the stripe, although in a few cases the simple colouring of a coat or pair of breeches is relieved with a flame-like motif, as shown in the design for the Dandy. The setting is a model of composition and of the difficult art of expressing much in the simplest terms.   No realistic representation of a Spanish landscape could bring home so forcibly the glare and heat of that land as do these white shapes, scored with grey and silhouetted against a patch of blue sky.

Costumes for the dancers of the "Pas de Deux"

Setting for the ballet in "Le Astuzie Femminili," Scene III.   Opera-ballet by Cimarosa,
orchestrated by O. Respighi, choreography by Leonide Massine.   Presented by the Diaghilev
Ballet Co., Royal Opera, Covent Garden, London, 1920.

The two costumes are delightful for their air of gaiety and fantasy.   As designs they show ingenious adaptation of eighteenth-century *Chinoiserie*, with such unusual features as cameo decorations connected with pom-poms (in the case of the man) and the combination of petal forms and tassels (in the case of the woman).   The scene, which suggests a panorama of Rome by moonlight, makes a romantic background for the costumes.

Costume for the young Buffoon's Wife.

Costume for the Old Buffoon.

Backcloth for " Chout " (The Buffoon).   Ballet with music by S. Prokofiev, choreography by T. Slavinsky and
M. Larionov.   Presented by the Diaghilev Ballet, Paris, 1921.

Another example of Larionov's fertility of decorative invention and fantasy of design.   Here art woven round Russian folklore is expressed in terms of the modernist school.   Note the unusual use of letters of varying size as an important element of the whole design.

Top—The Ostrich (left), The Bathing-Girl from Trouville (right). Below—The General (left), The Photographer (right).

Jean Hugo. Costumes for "Les Mariés de la Tour Eiffel." Ballet by Jean Cocteau, music by The Six, choreography by Jean Borlin. Presented by Rolf de Maré's Ballets Suédois, Théâtre des Champs-Elysées, Paris, 1921.

Andrée Parr.   Costumes for " L'Homme et Son
Désir."   Plastic poem by Paul Claudel, music by
Darius Milhaud, choreography by Jean Borlin.

Presented by Rolf de Maré's Ballets Suédois,
Théâtre des Champs-Elysées, Paris, 1921.

Scenes from " L'Oiseau de Feu." Settings and costumes designed by Natalia Goncharova. Originally produced for the Diaghilev Ballet Co., 1922, these photographs are from the revival, as presented by Col. W. de Basil's Ballets Russes. Ballet by Michel Fokine, music by Igor Stravinsky, choreography by M. Fokine.

Fernand Léger. Cubist setting and costumes for "Skating Rink." Ballet by R. Canudo, music by A. Honegger, choreography by Jean Borlin.

Presented by Rolf de Maré's Ballets Suédois, Théâtre des Champs-Elysées, Paris, 1922.

96

Paul Colin.   Setting for " Sculpture Nègre."   Dance executed and arranged by Jean Borlin.

*Andrée Parr.   Setting for " L'Homme et son Désir."   Plastic Poem by Paul Claudel, music by Darius Milhaud,
choreography by Jean Borlin.   Rolf de Maré's Ballets Suédois, Théâtre des Champs-Elysées, Paris, 1921.*

Gerald Murphy. Setting and costumes for "Within the Quota." The setting is a giant reproduction of an American "daily." The characters represented are: The Coloured Gentleman, The Immigrant, The World's Sweetheart, The Cow-boy. Ballet by G. Murphy, music by Cole Porter, choreography by Jean Borlin. Rolf de Maré's Ballets Suédois, Théâtre des Champs-Elysées, Paris, 1923.

Fernand Léger.   Costumes and cubist setting for " La Création du Monde."   Ballet by B. Cendrars, music by Darius Milhaud, choreography by Jean Borlin.   Presented by Rolf de Maré's Ballets Suédois, Théâtre des Champs-Elysées, Paris, 1923.

Irène Lagut.   Back-cloth for " Les Mariés de la Tour Eiffel."   Ballet by Jean Cocteau, music by The Six, choreography by Jean Borlin.   Presented by Rolf de Maré's Ballets Suédois, Théâtre des Champs-Elysées, Paris, 1921.

Giorgio di Chirico.   Setting for "La Jarre."   Ballet by L. Pirandello, music by A. Casella, choreography by Jean Borlin.   Presented by Rolf de Maré's Ballets Suédois, Théâtre des Champs-Elysées, Paris, 1924.

Hélène Perdriat.   Setting for " Marchand d'Oiseaux."   Ballet with music by Germaine Tailleferre, choreography by Jean Borlin.   Presented by Rolf de Maré's Ballets Suédois, Théâtre des Champs-Elysées, Paris, 1923.   Above, two costumes for " Marchand d'Oiseaux "—The Bird Vendor (left), The Younger Sister (right).

Natalia Goncharova. Setting for "Noces," Scene III, and two costumes. The men and women dancers each wear a stylised peasant dress of uniform design. Ballet with theme and music by I. Stravinsky. Presented by the Diaghilev Ballet Co., Gaité-Lyrique, Paris, 1923.

Scene from " Le Train Bleu." Setting by H. Laurens. Costumes by Chanel. Ballet by Jean Cocteau, music by Darius Milhaud, choreography by Bronislava Nijinska. Presented by the Diaghilev Ballet Co., Théâtre des Champs-Elysées, Paris, 1924.

Scene from " Les Biches." Setting and costumes by Marie Laurencin. Ballet with music by Francis Poulenc, choreography by Bronislava Nijinska. Presented by the Diaghilev Ballet Co., Théâtre de Monte Carlo, 1924.

Photo. : The Times, London

Francis Picabia.   Setting for " Relâche."   Ballet by F. Picabia, music by Erik Satie, production by F. Picabia, choreography by Jean Borlin.   Presented by Rolf de Maré's Ballets Suédois, Théâtre des Champs-Elysées, Paris, 1924.

Francis Picabia.   Curtain for " Relâche."   The names were painted in transparent colours, lit from behind, and made to flicker by inserting a flasher in the electric circuit, thus giving the effect of electric night-signs.

Michel Larionov. Setting for "Renard." Ballet with theme and music by I. Stravinsky. First version, with choreography by Bronislava Nijinska. Presented by Diaghilev Ballet Co., Théâtre National de l'Opéra, Paris, 1922. (Collection of A. Tomiline, Paris.)

Natalia Goncharova. Act-drop for "La Foire de Sorochinsk." Opera-ballet with music by Mussorgsky. Presented by Opéra et Ballet Privés de Paris, Théâtre des Champs-Elysées, 1926. (Collection of O. Rosenfeld, Paris.)

Photo.: *Henri Manuel, Paris*

Scene and costumes from " La Chatte." Constructivist setting by Gabo and Pevsner. The scenery and costumes are made of talc, a material with many attractive possibilities on account of its lightness, transparency, flexibility, and power to reflect light. Ballet by Sobeka, music by Henri Sauguet, choreography by George Balanchine. Presented by the Diaghilev Ballet Co., Prince's Theatre, London, 1927.

Nicholas Remisov. Setting for " The Tragedy of the Cello." Ballet with music by A. Tansman, choreography by Adolph Bolm, 1927.

Violin costume in " L'Orchestre en Liberté." Ballet with music by H. Sauveplan, choreography by Serge Lifar. Presented at Théâtre National de l'Opéra, Paris, 1931.

Photo.: Lipnitzki, Paris

Nicholas Remisov. Costume for a Violin in " The Tragedy of the Cello."

Jean Berain. Costume for a Musician. Example of 17th *century treatment of musical instruments as decorative elements for a dancer's costume.*

Alexandre Benois.   Setting for "Les Noces de Psyche et L'Amour."—Apotheosis.   Ballet to music by Bach, choreography by Bronislava Nijinska.   Ballet Ida Rubinstein, Opéra, Paris, 1928. Alexandre Benois.   Curtain for "Le Coq D'Or."   Théâtre National de l'Opéra, Paris, 1927.

Costumes for " Les Noces de Psyche et l'Amour."   *Ballet with music by Bach, choreography by Bronislava Nijinska.*   *Presented by Ballet Ida Rubinstein, Théâtre National de l'Opéra, Paris, 1928.*

Alexandre Benois.   *Costumes for " La Bien Aimée."*   *Ballet by A. Benois, music by Schubert and Liszt, choreography by Bronislava Nijinska.*   *Presented by Ballet Ida Rubinstein, Théâtre National de l'Opéra, Paris, 1928.*

Charles Martin.   Costumes for " Le Rustre Imprudent."   Ballet with choreography by Leo Staats.
Presented at Théâtre National de l'Opéra, Paris, 1931. (By courtesy of the Musée de l'Opéra).

Giorgio di Chirico.   Costumes for " La Jarre."   Ballet by L. Pirandello, music by A. Casella, choreography
by Jean Borlin.   Presented by Rolf de Maré's Ballets Suédois, Théâtre des Champs-Elysées, Paris, 1924.

*William Chappell. Costumes for "Capriol Suite."
Ballet to music by Peter Warlock, choreography by
Frederick Ashton. Presented by Ballet Rambert,
Lyric Theatre, Hammersmith, London, 1930.*

*Above, Costume for "Lysistrata"—A Wife. Ballet
to music by S. Prokofiev, choreography by Antony
Tudor. Presented by Ballet Rambert, Mercury
Theatre, London, 1932.*

*Left, William Chappell. Costume for "Bar Aux
Folies-Bergères"—The Barmaid. Ballet to music
by Chabrier, choreography by Ninette de Valois.
Ballet Rambert, Mercury Theatre, London, 1934.*

Scenes from "The Red Poppy," Act III, Scene I, and, below, Act I.   Settings and costumes by B. Erbstein.   Ballet by M. T. Kurilko, music by R. M. Glière, choreography by F. V. Lopukhov.   Presented by Soviet State Ballet.

Photo.: Crimella, Milan

Scenes from " Belkis, Queen of Sheba," Act I and, below, Act II.   Settings and costumes by Nicholas Benois. Ballet by C. Guastalla, music by O. Respighi, choreography by Leonide Massine.   Scala Theatre, Milan, 1932.

Georges Annenkov. Settings for " Les Comédiens Jaloux." Scene II, and, below, Scene I. Ballet based on Molière's play, with choreography by Bronislava Nijinska. Presented by La Nijinska's Théâtre de la Danse, Théâtre de l'Opéra, Paris, 1932.

Georges Annenkov.   Settings for " Variations," Part I, and, below, Part II.   Ballet in 3 parts, with choreography by Bronislava Nijinska.   Presented by La Nijinska's Théâtre de la Danse, Théâtre de l'Opéra Comique, Paris, 1932.

Michel Larionov. Scene model of constructivist setting for " Sur le Borysthène," with two costumes by Natalia Goncharova. Ballet with music by S. Prokofiev, choreography by Serge Lifar. Presented at the Théâtre National de l'Opéra, Paris, 1932. (By courtesy of the Musée l'Opéra, Paris).

Photo.: Raoul Barba, Monte Carlo

Scene from " Jeux d'Enfants." Setting and costumes by Joan Miro. Ballet by B. Kochno, music by G. Bizet, choreography by Leonide Massine. Les Ballets Russes de Monte Carlo, Théâtre de Monte Carlo, 1932.

Scene from " Ode." Setting by Pavel Tchelitchev. Ballet by B. Kochno, music by N. Nabokov, choreography by Leonide Massine. Diaghilev Ballet Co., His Majesty's Theatre, London, 1928.

Photo.: Lipnitzki, Paris

*Scenes from " Kuruc Fairy Tale," Act II, and, below, Act I.   Settings and costumes designed by Gusztav
Oláh.   Ballet by Zsolt Harsányi, music by Zoltán Kodály, choreography by Aurel Millos and Rezsö Brada.
Presented by Royal Hungarian State Ballet, Royal Opera House, Budapest, 1935.*

Photos : Vajda M. Pal, Budapest

Guzstav Oláh.   Costumes for " Kuruc Fairy Tale."   Ballet by Zsolt Harsányi, music by Zoltán Kodály, choreo-graphy by Aurel Millos and Rezsö Brada.   Royal Hungarian State Ballet, Royal Opera House, Budapest, 1935.

William Chappell. Costumes for " High Yellow." Ballet with music by Spike Hughes, choreography by Buddy Bradley and Frederick Ashton. Presented by Camargo Society, Savoy Theatre, London, 1932.

Vanessa Bell. Setting for " High Yellow." (In the collection of John V. Trevor).

V. V. Dmitriev.   Settings for " The Flames of Paris," Acts III and IV.   Ballet by N. D. Volkov and V. V. Dmitriev, music by B. V. Asafiev, choreography by V. I. Vynonen.   Presented by Soviet State Ballet, 1932.

Gwendolen Raverat.   Setting for " Job."   Masque for Dancing by Geoffrey Keynes, music by Vaughan Williams, choreography by Ninette de Valois. Presented by Camargo Society, Cambridge Theatre, London, 1931.   (In the collection of Geoffrey Keynes, Esq., London).

Nadia Benois. Setting for " Dark Elegies."   Ballet to music by Mahler, choreography by Antony Tudor. Presented by Ballet Rambert, Duchess Theatre, London, 1937.

Mitislav Dobuzhinsky. (Above) Two costumes for " La Belle au Bois Dormant "—The Blue Bird and A Duchess. Ballet by M. Petipa, music by P. I. Tchaikovsky, choreography by Marius Petipa. Revival as presented by Lithuanian Ballet, Kovno. (Below) costume for " Prince Igor "—Polovtsian Dancer. Revival as presented by Lithuanian Ballet, Kovno. Costume for " La Belle au Bois Dormant "—Carabosse.

Titina Rota.   Costumes for " The Birds."—The Cuckoo (left), The Cock (right).

M. Vellani-Marchi.   Setting for " The Birds."   Ballet by C. Guastalla, music by O. Respighi, choreography by Cia Fornaroli. Presented by Italian Chamber Ballet, San Remo, 1933.

Sophie Fedorovich.   Setting and costumes for " Les Masques."   Ballet with music by Francis Poulenc, choreography by Frederick Ashton.   Presented by Ballet Rambert, Mercury Theatre, London, 1933.

Photo. : Maurice Seymour, Chicago

Scene from " Choreartium."   Settings and costumes by Constantin Terechkovich and Eugene Lourie.   Ballet to music by Brahms, choreography by Leonide Massine.   Presented by Les Ballets Russes de Monte Carlo, Alhambra Theatre, London, 1933.

Photo. : Raoul Barba, Monte Carlo

Scene from " Les Présages."   Setting and costumes by André Masson.   Ballet by L. Massine, music by P. I. Tchaikovsky, choreography by Leonide Massine.   Presented by Les Ballets Russes de Monte Carlo, Théâtre de Monte Carlo, 1933.

Scene from " Scuola di Ballo."   Setting and costumes by the Comte Etienne de Beaumont.   Ballet by L. Massine, music by Boccherini, choreography by Leonide Massine.   Presented by Les Ballets Russes de Monte Carlo, Théâtre de Monte Carlo, 1933.

Photos.: Raoul Barba, Monte Carlo

Scene from " Le Beau Danube."   Setting by Vladimir Polunin after Constantin Guys.   Ballet by L. Massine, music by Johann Strauss, choreography by Leonide Massine.   Revival, Les Ballets Russes de Monte Carlo, 1933.

139

Two scenes from " The Three Fat Men."   Act I, Scene II, and Act III, Scene I.   Settings by B. A. Matrunin.
Ballet by I. Olecha, music by V. A. Oransky, choreography by I. A. Moiseyev.   Presented by Soviet State Ballet.

Two scenes from " Magyar Abrandok," (Hungarian Fantasy), Acts II and III.   Setting and costumes by Zoltan Fülop and Gusztav Oláh, respectively. Ballet by L. Markus, music by Liszt, choreography by Jan Cieplinsky. Presented by Royal Hungarian State Ballet, Royal Opera House, Budapest, 1933.

Photos.: Vajda M. Pal, Budapest

Mitislav Dobuzhinsky. Setting for " Arlequinade," and two costumes, for Harlequin and Columbine. Ballet with music by Richard Drigo. Lithuanian Ballet, State Theatre, Kovno.

William Chappell. Two costumes, for Zi'Dima (left) and Nela (right), and back-cloth for " The Jar." Ballet by L. Pirandello, music by A. Casella, choreography by Ninette de Valois. Revival, as presented by Vic-Wells Ballet, Sadler's Wells Theatre, London, 1934.

F. F. Fedorovsky.   Costumes for the Polovtsian Dances in " Prince Igor."   Opera by Borodin, production by Baratov.   Presented at the Bolshoy Theatre, Moscow, 1934.

F. F. FEDOROVSKY

Scene from " Prince Igor "—Polovtsian Dances.   Setting by F. F. Fedorovsky.

Costume for Abderam.

Costume for Spanish Dance—Panaderos.

*Mitislav Dobuzhinsky.   Costume designs for Raymonda.   Ballet by
L. Pashkov and M. Petipa, music by A. Glazunov, choreography by Marius
Petipa.   Revival, as presented by Lithuanian State Ballet, Kovno, 1934.*

Mitislav Dobuzhinsky.   Setting for " Raymonda."   Act 1, Scene II.

George Sheringham. Setting for " The Lord of Burleigh." Ballet to music by Mendelssohn, choreography by Frederick Ashton. Presented by the Camargo Society, London, 1931. (In the collection of John V. Trevor).

George Sheringham. Setting for " Pan," ballet not yet given. (In the collection of Helen Gardiner, M.V.O., and Patience Osburn).

148

Hugh Stevenson.   Above ; Costume for " Gala Performance "—La Fille de Terpsichore, and " Soirée Musicale "—Tyrolien.
Both presented by The London Ballet, Toynbee Hall Theatre, 1938, and Palladium Theatre, London, 1938.   Below ; Costume
for " Soirée Musicale "—Tarantella, and " Gala Performance "—La Reine de la Danse.

Photo.: F. W. Debenham, London

Scene from " The Gods Go A-Begging." Setting and costumes by Hugh Stevenson. Ballet to music by Handel, arranged by Sir Thomas Beecham, choreography by Ninette de Valois. Presented by Vic-Wells Ballet, Sadler's Wells Theatre, London, 1934.

" Cotillon." Setting and costumes by Christian Bérard. Ballet with music by Chabrier, choreography by George Balanchine. Ballets Russes de Monte Carlo, Théâtre de Monte Carlo, 1932.

Photo.: Raoul Barba, Monte Carlo

Motley. Setting for " The Haunted Ballroom," and costume (The Stranger Player). Ballet with music by Geoffrey Toye, choreography by Ninette de Valois. Presented by the Vic-Wells Ballet, Sadler's Wells Theatre, London, 1934.

*Sophie Fedorovich.   Costumes for " Mephisto Valse "—Mephisto, Marguerite.   Ballet with music by Liszt,
choreography by Frederick Ashton.   Ballet Rambert, Duke of York's Theatre, London, 1935.*

*Scene from " Le Baiser de la Fée."   Setting by Bassadoua.   Ballet with music by I. Stravinsky, choreography
by Bronislava Nijinska.   Presented at Colon Theatre, Buenos Aires, 1932.*

William Chappell. Project for setting for " Giselle," and two costumes—Prince Albrecht (left), and Giselle, 2nd act (right). Ballet by V. de Saint-Georges and T. Gautier, music by A. Adam, choreography by J. Perrot and J. Coralli. Revival, presented by Vic-Wells Ballet, Sadler's Wells Theatre, London.

P. M. Larthe.   Costumes for " Icare "—Icare, Dedale.   Ballet by Serge Lifar, rhythms by S. Lifar, orchestrated by J. E. Szyfer, choreography by Serge Lifar.   Presented Théâtre Nationale de l'Opéra, Paris, 1935.   (Courtesy of the Musée de l'Opéra, Paris).

Photo.: *A. F. Vaughan, London*

Scene from " Beach."   Setting and costumes by Raoul Dufy.   Ballet by R. Kerdyk, music by Jean Françaix, choreography by Leonide Massine.   Presented by Ballets Russes de Monte Carlo, Théâtre de Monte Carlo, 1933.

Photo.: Rauol Barba, Monte Carlo

Scene from " Casse Noisette," Act I, Scene II.   Ballet with music by P. I. Tchaikovsky.   Revival, with choreography by Boris Romanov, as presented by René Blum's Ballets de Monte Carlo, Alhambra Theatre, London, 1936.

Photo.: F. W. Debenham, London

Scene from " The Nursery Suite." Setting by William Chappell. Ballet with music by Sir Edward Elgar, choreography by Ninette de Valois.   Vic-Wells Ballet, Sadler's Wells Theatre, London.

Mitislav Dobuzhinsky. Setting for " Les Sylphides." Ballet to music by Chopin, choreography by Michel Fokine. Revival, as presented by Lithuanian Ballet, Alhambra Theatre, London, 1935.

Mitislav Dobuzhinsky. Setting for " The Dwarf Grenadier." Ballet with music by H. Preston, choreography by Nicholas Zverev. Presented by Lithuanian Ballet, Alhambra Theatre, London, 1935.

Scene from "Coppélia," Act II. Settings and costumes designed by Mitislav Dobuzhinsky, book by C. Nuitter and A. Saint-Léon, music by L. Delibes, choreography by Nicholas Zverev. Revival, as presented by René Blum's Ballets de Monte Carlo, Alhambra Theatre, London, 1936.

Photo.: Raoul Barba, Monte Carlo

Scene from " Aubade." Settings and costumes by A. Cassandre, music by F. Poulenc, choreography by George Balanchine. Revival, presented by René Blum's Ballets de Monte Carlo, Alhambra, 1936.

Coll.: Harold Rubin

Setting for " Gala Performance," Scene II.   Ballet by Antony Tudor, produced 1938

Setting for Giselle, Act. II.

Hugh Stevenson.   Back-cloth and two costume designs for " Le Jardin aux Lilas."   Ballet by Antony Tudor, music by Chausson, choreography by Antony Tudor.   Ballet Rambert, Mercury Theatre, London, 1936.

Fernand Léger.   Two settings for " David Triomphant," Scenes I and II.   Ballet to music by Debussy and Mussorgsky, and rhythms by Serge Lifar, orchestrated by V. Rieti, choreography by Serge Lifar. Presented at Théâtre de la Maison Internationale des Etudiants, Paris, 1936.

Phyllis Dolton.   Costume for " Espagnol " (Dance composed by Anton Dolin).   Costume for ballet—1815 period.

Phyllis Dolton.   Costume for " The Nightingale and the Rose "—The Young Girl.   Costume for a grotesque Chinese dance.

Pavel Tchelitchev. Costume for a Fury (Act II) and setting for "Orpheus." Opera-ballet by Gluck, choreography by George Balanchine. Presented by American Ballet Co., New York, 1936.

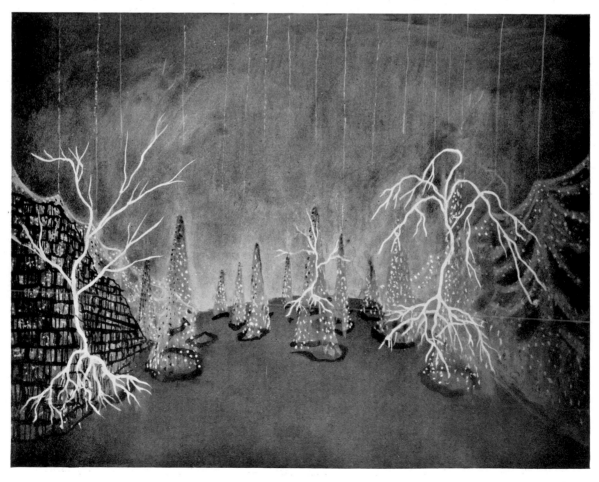

Bernard Meninsky. Back-cloth for " David." Ballet by P. Vanda, music by Maurice Jacobson, choreography by Keith Lester. Presented by Markova-Dolin Ballet, Duke of York's Theatre, London, 1936.

Bernard Meninsky. Back-cloth for " Death in Adagio." Ballet by Keith Lester, music by Scarlatti, choreography by Keith Lester. Presented by Markova-Dolin Ballet, King's Theatre, Southsea, England, 1936.

Two scenes (VIII and III) from " The Love of the Three Pomegranates."   Setting by Nicholas Benois.   Ballet with music by G. C. Sonzogno, choreography by Michel Fokine.   Presented at Scala Theatre, Milan, 1936.

Photos: Crimella, Milan

Scene from " Csárdajelenet " (Inn Scene). Setting and costumes designed by Zoltan Fülöp. Ballet by Viktor Lányi, music by Jenö Hubay, choreography by Gyula Harangozò. Presented by Royal Hungarian State Ballet, Royal Opera House, Budapest, 1936.

Scene from " Szent Fáklya " (The Holy Torch). Setting and Costumes by Zoltan Fülöp. Ballet by Elsa von Galafres, music by Ernst von Dohnányi, choreography by Elsa von Galafres and Rezsö Brada. Presented by Royal Hungarian State Ballet, Royal Opera House, Budapest, 1934.

Photos.: Vajda M. Pal, Budapest

Mitislav Dobuzhinsky. Setting and two costumes for "Casse-Noisette," Act II. Revival, as presented by Vic-Wells Ballet, Sadler's Wells Theatre, London, 1936.

Photo. : Raoul Barba, Monte Carlo

Scene from "L'Epreuve d'Amour". Setting and costumes by André Derain. Ballet by A. Derain and M. Fokine, music by Mozart, choreography by Michel Fokine. Presented by René Blum's Ballets de Monte Carlo, Théâtre de Monte Carlo, 1936.

V. V. Dmitriev.   Two settings for " Lost Illusions."   Ballet based on Balzac's " Illusions Perdues," with music by Asafiev.   Presented by Soviet State Ballet.

I. Rabinovich.   Two scene models for " La Belle au Bois Dormant."   Ballet by Marius Petipa, music by Tchaikovsky, choreography by Marius Petipa.   Revival, as presented by the Soviet State Ballet.

Scene from " Don Juan."   Proscenium and curtain designed by Mariano Andreù.   Ballet by Eric Allatini and Michel Fokine, music by Gluck, choreography by Michel Fokine.   Presented by René Blum's Ballets de Monte Carlo, Alhambra Theatre, London, 1936.   Dances and mimed scenes are given in front of the curtain, which is drawn aside to reveal the main scene.

Mariano Andreù.   Costumes for " Don Juan."   Ballet by Eric Allatini and Michel Fokine, to music by Gluck, choreography by Michel Fokine.   Presented by René Blum's Ballets de Monte Carlo, Alhambra Theatre, London, 1936.

Mariano Andreù. Setting and costumes for "Jota Aragonesa." Ballet to music by Glinka, choreography by Michel Fokine. Revival, as presented by René Blum's Ballets de Monte Carlo, Coliseum Theatre, London, 1937.

George Kirsta.   Setting and two costumes for " La Bien Aimée."   Ballet by A. Benois, music by Schubert and Liszt, choreography by Bronislava Nijinska.   Revival, as presented by the Markova-Dolin Ballet, King's Theatre, Hammersmith, London, 1937.

Photo.: F. S[

Types of cos[
Designed b[
in Space.

William Chappell. Setting and two costumes for " Les Patineurs."   Ballet to music by Meyerbeer, choreography by Frederick Ashton.   Presented by Vic-Wells Ballet, Sadler's Wells Theatre, London, 1937.

Scene from " Le Baiser de la Fée."   Setting by Alice Halicka.   Ballet with Music by I. Stravinsky, choreography
by George Balanchine. Presented by American Ballet Co., New York, 1937. Above, two costumes by Alice
Halicka for the same ballet.

Angelo Pinto.   Setting for " Barn Dance," and three costumes (The City Slicker, The Light Maiden and The Deacon).   Ballet by Catherine Littlefield, music by J. Powell, D. Guion, and L. M. Gottschalk, choreography by Catherine Littlefield.   Presented by Philadelphia Ballet Co., Hippodrome, London, 1937.

Photo. : Damgaard, Copenhagen

Scene from " La Veuve dans le Miroir." Setting and Costumes by Kjeld Abell, ballet by K. Abell, music by B. Christensen, choreography by Börge Ralov. Presented at Theatre Royal, Copenhagen.

Scene from " Anna Anna, or The Seven Capital Sins." Setting and Costumes by Svend Johannsen, ballet based on Poems by Bert Brecht, music by Kurt Weill, choreography by Harold Lander. Presented at Theatre Royal, Copenhagen.

Photo. : Mydtskov, Copenhagen

Dimitri Bouchêne. Setting and Costumes for " Les Elements." Ballet to music by J. S. Bach, choreography by Michel Fokine. Presented by René Blum's Ballets de Monte Carlo, Coliseum Theatre, London, 1937.

Christian Bérard. Setting for " The Seventh Symphony," Part III. Ballet by Leonide Massine to Beethoven's Seventh
Symphony, choreography by Leonide Massine. Presented by Ballets Russe de Monte Carlo, Théâtre de Monte Carlo, 1938.

Paul Colin. Above: Backcloth for " Rugby." Ballet presented at Casino de Paris, Paris, 1931.
Below: Setting for " Finances." Ballet presented by Ballets de Paris, 1937.

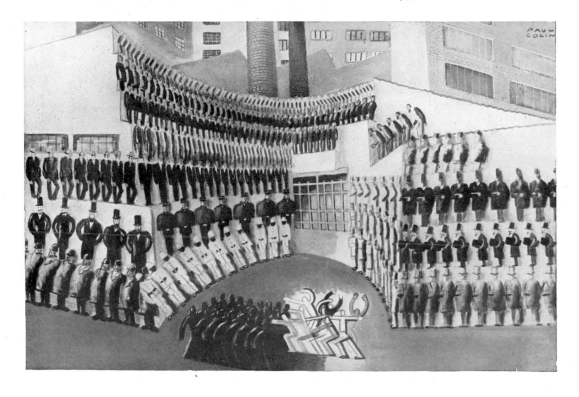

Scenes I and II from " Perhaps To-morrow !"   Setting by Aladár Olgyay.   Costumes by Klára
Szunyogh-Tüdös and Tivadar Márk.   Ballet by I. Juhász, music by J. Kenessey, choreography by Gyula
Harangozó.   Presented at Metropolitan Art Theatre, Budapest, 1937.

Photos.: Vajda M. Pal, Budapest

Scene from " Csongor és Tünde." Setting and costumes by Gusztav Oláh.   Ballet by L. Márkus, music by L. Weiner, choreography by Jan Cieplinsky.   Presented by Royal Hungarian State Ballet, Royal Opera House, Budapest, 1930.

Scene from " Jószi the Wise."   Setting by Zoltan Fülöp.   Ballet by E. Mohacsi and L. Márkus, music by G. Kosa, choreography by Jan Cieplinsky.   Royal Hungarian State Ballet, Budapest, 1933.

Photos.: Vajda M. Pál, Budapest

Scene from " Little Johnny in Top-Boots." Setting by Zoltan Fülöp. Costumes by Gusztav Oláh. Ballet by E. Clementis, music by J. Kenessey, choreography by Gyula Harangozó. Presented by Royal Hungarian State Ballet, Royal Opera House, Budapest, 1937.

The same. "Night-time." As the light dims, a blue cloth is lowered which, lit from behind, ushers in the moon and stars ; simultaneously the wings are moved closer in.

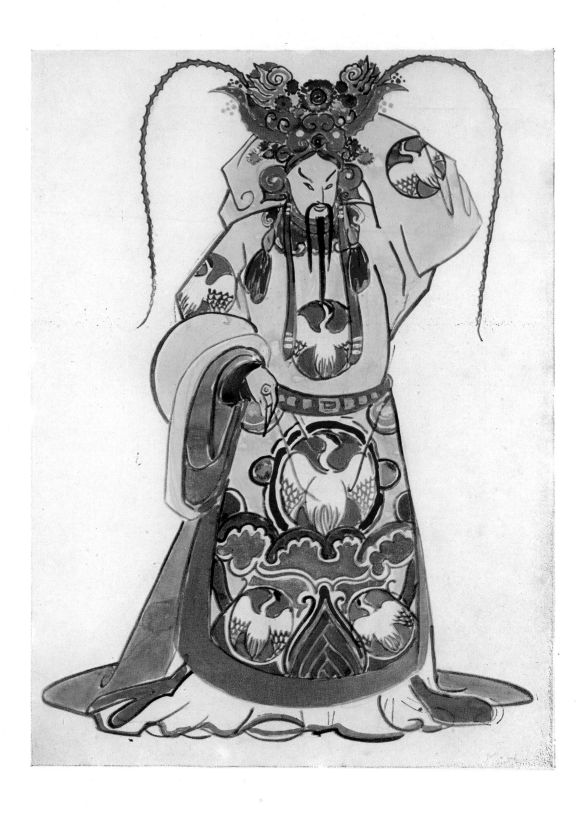

*Costume for the Emperor of China in " The Emperor and the Nightingale," opera-ballet, adapted by
Michael Martin-Harvey from the well-known story by Hans Andersen, with music by Kennedy Russell.
Not yet produced.*

Oliver Messel.   Setting, Scene I, and costumes for "Comus," masque after John Milton, to music by Henry Purcell, choreography by Robert Helpmann.   Presented by Sadler's Wells Ballet, New Theatre, London, 1942.

Costume for Comus, Scene II.   *Costume for Male Dancer in the Rout.*

Ludolf Liberts.   Setting for Act III, and two costumes for " The Triumph of Love."   Ballet by Voldemārs
Komisārs, music by Jānis Mediņš, choreography by Osvalds Lēmanis.   Presented by Latvian Ballet, Riga, 1935.

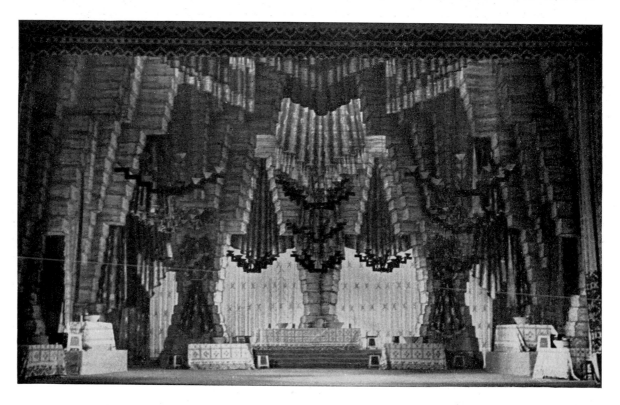

Ludolf Liberts. Settings for Prologue (above), Act I (centre), and Act II of " La Belle au Bois Dormant," ballet by Marius Petipa, music by P. I. Tchaikovsky, choreography by Marius Petipa. As presented by Latvian Ballet, Riga, 1929.

Salvador Dali.   Three costumes for " Labyrinth."   These three groups have been chosen to show the application of surrealist principles to costume design.

Four Costumes for " Bacchanale."   *Three Costumes for " Labyrinth."*

SALVADOR DALI

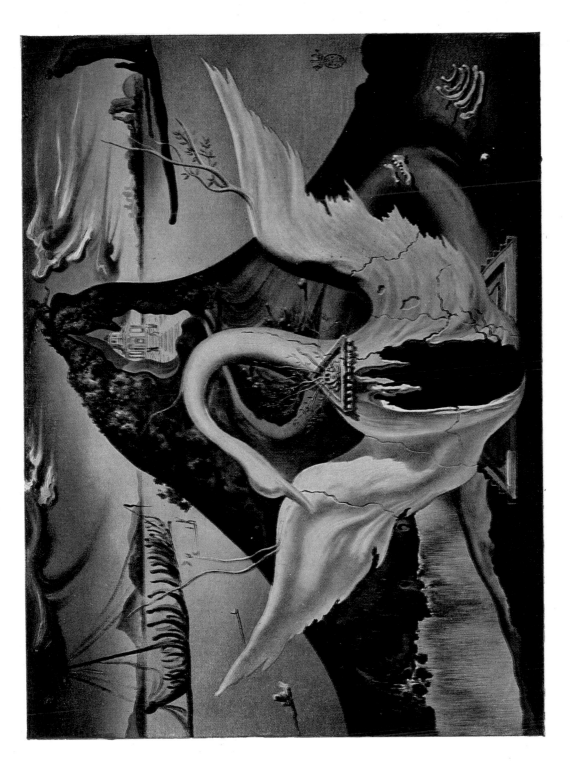

Salvador Dali.   Back-cloth for "Bacchanale."   Ballet by Salvador Dali to music by Richard Wagner, choreography by Leonide Massine.
Presented by Ballets Russe de Monte Carlo, Metropolitan Opera House, New York, 1939.

Sophie Fedorovich.   Drop-curtain for " Horoscope."   Ballet with music by Constant Lambert, choreography by Ninette de Valois.   Presented by Vic-Wells Ballet, Sadler's Wells Theatre, London, 1938.

Photo.: Vajda M. Pal, Budapest

Gusztav Oláh.   Setting for " Salade," choreography by Gyula Harangozó.   Presented by Royal Hungarian State Ballet, Royal Hungarian Opera House, Budapest, 1939.

Nadia Benois. Setting and two costumes for " Lady into Fox." Ballet after novel by David Garnett, to music by Arthur Honegger, choreography by Andrée Howard. Presented by Ballet Rambert, Mercury Theatre, London, 1939.

Costume for Mrs. Tebrick.   *Costume for Mrs. Tebrick as Fox.*

The action of the ballet requires the metamorphosis of Mrs. Tebrick into a Fox to be achieved within the space of a momentary black-out. The artist solved this problem in a very ingenious manner. The dancer first dons rust-coloured fleshings with black feet, the tail is made of a length of ruffled muslin. Over this the dancer wears a dress with a bustle typical of the Victorian era. At the back of the dress is a deep pocket into which the fox's tail is inserted. Black footless stockings are drawn over the legs of the fleshings. When the dancer changes, she pulls off the detachable bang with bow so that the wig suggests the pointed tips of the fox's ears, the dress is unzipped, the black footless stockings drawn off, and the metamorphosis is complete.

S. E. Alladzhalov. Settings for Act II, Scene II (above), and Act I of "Happiness." Ballet by G. A. Ovanesian, music by Aram Khachaturian, choreography by E. E. Arbatov (Gagubian). Presented at Armenian Festival of Folk Art, Moscow, 1940.

*P. Williams.   Setting for " Romeo and Juliet."   Ballet after Shakespeare's play, music by Sergey Prokofiev,
choreography by L. Lavrovsky.   Presented : Kirov State Theatre of Opera and Ballet, Leningrad, 1940.*

Coll.: *John Doughty*

*Roger Furse.   Setting for Scene III (above), and Act-drop for Scenes II and VI of " The Prospect Before Us."
Ballet by Ninette de Valois, to music by William Boyce, choreography by Ninette de Valois.   Presented by
Vic-Wells Ballet, Sadler's Wells Theatre, London, 1940.*

Coll.: John Doughty

Costume for a Dancer in Practice Dress.

Costume for Mr. O'Reilly.

Costume for Mlle. Théodore.

Costume for M. Vestris.

Guy Sheppard.   Setting and two costumes for "Peter and the Wolf."   Ballet with music by Sergey Prokofiev, and choreography by Frank Staff.   Presented by Ballet Rambert, Arts Theatre, Cambridge, 1940.

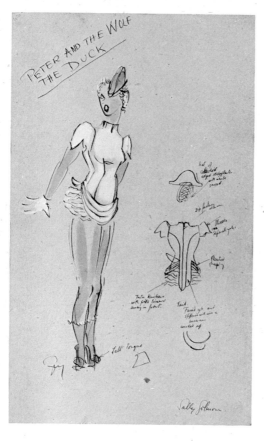

Costume for the Duck.

Costume for the Wolf.

(Left) Costume for Fadette—(Right)—Costume for a Dancer in " Jeu de la Rose."   Divertissement with theme by C. W. Beaumont to music by Johann Strauss, choreography by Molly Lake.   Presented by Ballet Guild, Rudolph Steiner Hall, London, 1941.

Costume for Landry.   *Costume for a Peasant Girl.*

Sylvia Green.   Costumes (top left and two below) for " La Petite Fadette," ballet in two acts by Deryck Lynham, after novel by George Sand, to music by Fauré, choreography by Molly Lake.   Presented by Ballet Guild, Arts Theatre, London, 1942.

Sophie Fedorovich. Back-cloth and two Costumes for " Dante Sonata." Ballet to music by Liszt, with choreography by Frederick Ashton. Presented by Vic-Wells Ballet, Sadler's Wells Theatre, London, 1940. Note the extreme simplicity of the back-cloth, the decoration of which is reminiscent of the calligraphic designs beloved of Chinese artists.

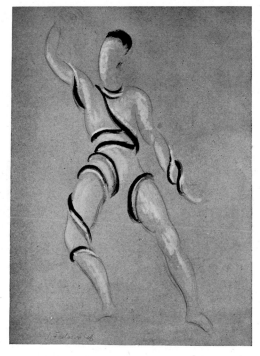

Costume for a Child of Darkness.   Costume for a Child of Light.

Coll.: John Doughty

Sophie Fedorovich.   Drop-curtain and settings for " Orpheus and Eurydice."   Opera-Ballet, with music by Gluck, choreography by Ninette de Valois.   Presented by Sadler's Wells Ballet, New Theatre, London, 1941. Drop-curtain for Act I, Scene 1 (above left).   Setting for Act II, Scene 2 (above right) ; in realisation, the mountain was replaced by draped gauze, similarly suspended by white cords.   Setting for Act I, Scene 1 (below left) ; the gauze is black, the cloth sky blue.   Act drop for Act I, Scene 2 (below right)—the entrance to Hades.

Paul Dupont.   Setting for " Frankie and Johnny."   Ballet by M. Blandford and J. Moross, with music by J. Moross and choreography by Ruth Page and Bentley Stone.   Great Northern Theatre, Chicago.   The ballet is based on the well-known song : " He was her man, but she done him wrong."

George Kirsta. Drop-curtain and Setting for " A Night on the Bare Mountain," ballet with
choreography by Catherine Dévillière, in " Sorotchintsi Fair," opera by Mussorgsky. As
presented at Savoy Theatre, London, 1941.

Costume for the Redcoat Devil.

Costume for Dancer in Gopak.

Costume for the Khivia Witch.

Costume for a Devil.

Salvador Dali.   Two settings for " Labyrinth."   Ballet by S. Dali to music by Franz Schubert, choreography by Leonide Massine.   Presented by Ballets Russe de Monte Carlo, Metropolitan Opera House, New York, 1941.

Leslie Hurry. Setting and two costumes for " Hamlet." Ballet after Shakespeare's play, to music by Tchaikovsky, choreography by Robert Helpmann. Presented by Sadler's Wells Ballet, New Theatre, London, 1942.

Costume for Hamlet.   *Costume for Ophelia.*

Julio Castellanos. Setting for " Don Domingo."   Ballet by Alfonso Reyes, after a story by Alarcon, music by Silvestre Revueltas, choreography by Leonide Massine, presented by Ballet Theatre, Palacio de Bellas Artes, Mexico City, 1942.

Alvin Colt.   Setting for " Slavonika."   Ballet by V. Psota, music by Antonin Dvorak, choreography by Vania Psota.   Presented by Ballet Theatre, 1941.

Roberto Montenegro.   Drop-curtain for "Coppélia."   Ballet by C. Nuitter and A. Saint-Léon, music by Leo Delibes, choreography by Simon Semenov, after Ivanov and Mérante.   Presented by the Ballet Theatre, 1942.

Marcel Vertes.   Setting for "Bluebeard," Act IV.   Ballet by M. Fokine, after opéra-bouffe by de Meilhac and Halévy, music by J. Offenbach, choreography by Michel Fokine.   Presented by Ballet Theatre, Palacio de Bellas Artes, Mexico City, 1941.

John Piper.   Settings for Scene V (above) and Scene I (below) of " The Quest."   Ballet by Doris Langley Moore after Spenser's " Færie Queene," music by William Walton, choreography by Frederick Ashton.   Presented by Sadler's Wells Ballet, New Theatre, London, 1943.